AUGUSTINIAN HUMANISM:

Studies in Human Bondage and Earthly Grace

James W. Woelfel
University of Kansas

University Press of America™

FOREWORD

Augustinian Humanism is a collection of closely-related essays which delineate and explore a humanistic perspective at least the broad outlines of which seem to me to be indicated by the knowledge we have of ourselves and the world. It is a humanism that draws upon and attempts to distill out in a general and "demythologized" way something of the perennial wisdom of some of the leading thinkers in Christian theology who might be called "Augustinians": Augustine himself, Luther, Calvin, Edwards, Kierkegaard, and Reinhold Niebuhr. The Augustinian themes which I transmute into a "secularized" framework are the radical creatureliness and deep bondage of our personal and social existence, and the decisive role of grace in healing and elevating that existence. Hence the subtitle of the book: _Studies in Human Bondage and Earthly Grace_. Elements of such a humanism can be found in a number of modern secular writers, and I am particularly indebted to Freud and the psychoanalytic tradition, Bertrand Russell, and Albert Camus. What I seek to do is to articulate such a "tragic humanism" with general and explicit reference to the Augustinian theological tradition, by way of showing the striking contemporary relevance of some of its great themes.

The Prologue, "A Belated Postscript to the Death of God," provides the personal and theological background to the book as a whole, finding in the sheer magnitude and fiendish diversity of gratuitous human suffering an insuperable personal obstacle to Christian faith. Chapter One, "'Essential' Calvinism as Contemporary Wisdom," is the programmatic essay: a comprehensive statement of an "Augustinan humanism" which sets the themes of the essays that comprise the body of the book.

Chapter Two, "Of Human Bondage: Augustinianism Old and New," examines the perplexing problem of what to make of the notions of freedom and responsibility within a context of the indefinitely large degree of biological and environmental shaping in human behavior, and attempts to resolve it by redefining freedom in terms of potentialities and providing a pragmatic justification of the crucial concept of responsibility. In Chapter Three, "Politics for Not-So-Rational Animals," I argue for a kind of political liberalism as the "humane realism" politically demanded by the irrationalities and unfreedom of the human condition, highlighting this view within the context of a critique of the beguiling superficiality of political libertarianism. Chapter Four, "Two Earthly Graces," translates the radical Augustinian emphasis on the supreme power andall-sufficiency of divine grace into the utter necessity of earthly graces for human living-secular as well as religious--in a world of suffering and bondage. I single out the graces of compassion and beauty for discussion: the former an essential dimension of an ethics arising from a realistic grasp of our condition, the latter a profound source of ecstasy and healing in human life.

Having begun with despair over the problem of God in the light of human bondage, I end with a certain groping, hopeful perplexity over the possibility of transcendence precisely by looking at our bondage from yet another perspective. In the Epilogue, "Charlie Citrine and the Argument from Absurdity," I draw again on the Augustinian tradition, this time by way of hesitantly grappling with the fact that even within a humanistic perspective one can and ought to be profoundly haunted by the possibility that we in our mysterious bondage and darkly enveloping cosmic environment may be far more than we know or suspect except through the terribly inadequate symbols of faith. Both the despair and the hope seem to me to belong to a humanism which tries to be sensitive to the whole puzzling complexity of human experience.

Some of the material in the essays that follow has appeared in article form. "A Belated Postscript to the Death of God" is a revised and expanded version of "The Death of God: A Belated Personal Postscript," copyright 1976 Christian Century Foundation, reprinted by permission from the December 29, 1976 issue of The Christian Century. Chapter Two, "Of Human Bondage: Augustinianism Old and New," incorporates most of the material in "Listening to B. F. Skinner," copyright 1977

Christian Century Foundation, reprinted by permission from the November 30, 1977 issue of The Christian Century. Chapter Three, "Politics for Not-So-Rational Animals," combines, in revised form, "We're Not Rational Animals: A Liberal Reply to Libertarianism," copyright 1973 Christian Century Foundation, reprinted by permission from the November 7, 1973 issue of The Christian Century; and "Author's Response: To Assure the Greatest Good for the Greatest Number," copyright 1974 Christian Century Foundation, reprinted by permission from the June 12-19, 1974 issue of The Christian Century. The Epilogue, "Charlie Citrine and the Argument from Absurdity," is a slightly revised and expanded version of an article with the same title, reprinted by permission from Religion in Life, Winter, 1978. Copyright 1978 by Abingdon. Excerpts from The Blood of the Lamb by Peter De Vries, copyright 1961 are reprinted by permission of the publisher, Little, Brown & Co. Material quoted from Humboldt's Gift by Saul Bellow, copyright 1975, is reprinted by permission from The Viking Press, Inc. The author gratefully acknowledges the granting of permission to use the above material by the publishers named.

I want also to express my appreciation to agencies and persons who have contributed in various ways to this book. Research on the project was supported by University of Kansas General Research allocations #3124-2038 and #3093-20-0038, awarded me in 1977 and 1978. An additional grant from the Small Grants portion of the General Research Fund supported the final typing of the book. I am grateful to Julie McLemore, my typist, who has been very patient and quietly efficient; and to Connie Ducey, former secretary of the Department of Philosophy, who with her usual skill smoothly set up the whole operation.

Various persons have stimulatingly and helpfully commented on the material that first appeared in article form: Owen Thomas, Professor of Theology at the Episcopal Divinity School; Joseph Fletcher, Professor of Medical Ethics at the University of Virginia Medical School; and Robert Bilheimer, Executive Director of the Institute for Ecumenical and Cultural Research--good friends, all-- corresponded spiritedly with me about the "death of

God" essay. In a brief conversation Robert McAtee Brown, Professor of Ecumenics and World Christianity at Union Theological Seminary, usefully related that essay to the haunting theological insights of Elie Wiesel. Mary Lenius of Chaska, Minnesota, wrote a creative and thoughtful poem in response to the same essay which hangs on my office wall. John Hospers, Professor of Philosophy at the University of Southern California and Libertarian Party candidate for President in 1972, wrote a defense of libertarian political philosphy in response to my article critiquing libertarianism (The Christian Century, vol. xci, no. 23, June 12-19, 1974, pp. 647-648), and my published rebuttal has been incorporated into the expanded essay "Politics for Not-So-Rational Animals." Rex Martin, former chairman of the Department of Philosophy, not only strongly supported my research in his official capacity but also took a personal interest in my work on B. F. Skinner, alerting me to articles on Skinner and engaging me in good dialogue. I am particularly grateful to my good friend Emily Russell, clinical social worker and a social sevices administrator with the Kansas Social and Rehabilitation Services, for many very stimulating conversations about the material in this book. With her knowledge and experience in psychology and mental health, she provided lively criticism, helpful information, and creative insight especially in connection with my work on Chapters One and Two. It goes without saying of course that none of the above persons should be held in any way responsible for the deficiencies in this collection of essays.

James W. Woelfel
Lawrence, Kansas

iv

CONTENTS

PROLOGUE

A BELATED POSTSCRIPT TO THE DEATH OF GOD

All the fun and games, the agonies and ecstasies, the caricatures and sober evaluations concerning the death of God theologies of the 'sixties have been tediously documented and are to a large degree out of mind in the 'seventies. I did my share of first welcoming the death-of-God theologians Altizer and Hamilton for "speaking to the condition" of skeptically-inclined and despairing theologians like myself, then scornfully dismissing their writings as theologically esoteric, puerile, reductionistic, and (ironically) not really in touch with the current religious Zeitgeist. Despite my skepticism, I never ceased hankering after transcendence, and so I enthusiastically welcomed the "recovery of transcendence" in theology that "gave us back God," restored us to multidimensionality, and made us in a way comfortable once again.

But here I am, more than ten years later, having waked up somewhat belatedly to discover that God has indeed died for me as well. There are crucial differences between my own recent experience of the death of God and the theologies of Altizer and Hamilton, and the differences perhaps point to the varieties even of this form of "religious experience." One difference is tonal: The necro-theologians of the 1960's were exultant; for me the experience is filled only with pathos and nostalgia. The other chief difference is etiological: Their problem was a relatively new phenomenon called secularization. Mine is an old and permanent specter called evil. What oppresses me sufficiently that God has not been able to survive it--and I am almost embarrassed to admit defeat by such a thoroughly well-worn issue--is that there is simply too much suffering. Dr. Bernard Rieux, the narrator of Camus's challenging statement on suffering called The Plague, sums it up with appropriate intensity and particularity. This world, he says, is "a scheme of things in which children are put to

1

torture."[1] It is a world in which, from many causes, children are too easily and too frequently stunted, warped, denied, deprived, abused, malnourished, diseased, shot, gassed, bombed, and generally robbed of their potentiality. What happens to children is a particularly graphic indicator of the depth of our human bondage to forces within ourselves and our planet.

It is not a sour Marcionism, "down on the world," that I have come to. Quite the contrary: There are many aspects of this life and this earth that I love sensually and cling to devotedly. I know full well that earth, so heedless of our personal welfare, also nurtures us remarkably and graces our lives with myriad beauties. I recognize that the unconscious which is the abysmal source of our earthly demons is also the dynamic ground of love and creativity which, together with our cognitive capacities, produces the truths and beauties and goodnesses of human life. I acknowledge that the social environments of family, race, class, education, work, culture, cult and nation are the inescapably human contexts that shape all our possibilities and achievements as well as our blindnesses and follies. My religious despair is not over finite existence as such; not over spatio-temporal limitations and interdependence in themselves. Nor is it even over the fact of challenges, obstacles, pain, and conflict as elements of finitude--elements which seem necessary to growth, relationship, morality, and health. My anguish is rather over the crushingly heavy burden of what seems to me non-sensical, gratuitous bondage. It is the sheer excess, the disproportion, of our human bondages and the absurdity resulting from this excess, the grotesque pointlessness of so much of it, that undermine my sense of ultimate meaning as transcendent willing purpose. Doctrines of a fall of humankind, original sin, and satanic power--whether historically or symbolically understood--fail to alleviate this brooding impression. They simply transpose the problem into another key and continue to beg the agonizing question posed to a sovereign divine purpose.

I have never ceased puzzling mightily over this old old "problem of evil" until, to adapt a line from Dr. Seuss, my puzzler is chronically sore. My incapacity to make sense out of the world as the creation of a personally caring Creator because of the magnitude of suffering is, to extend the metaphor, a long-festering sore that simply will not heal. Theologically it is somewhat awkward to be still bleeding over the issue when everyone else has gone on to other more exciting things. (I suppose even what I am doing in this essay could be construed as belonging to the recently popular "theology as autobiography" genre!) Chalk it up if you wish to a poverty of experience and imagination: I am perfectly willing to grant that it may indeed be so.

Still, there it is, my tiresome old wound, and its pain will not go away. I spent a major portion of my book Borderland Christianity[2] trying to salve the affliction theologically while clinging to some semblance of a Christian perspective that preserved the element of transcendence in its God-talk. But one thing I affirmed there with all the earnestness and energy I could muster: A being who creates this universe ex nihilo is inescapably responsible for its features, and to call such a being "love" I could not help but find incomprehensible and offensive. I suggested, without choosing among, some alternative views of God that in varying ways preserved the divine love at the expense of divine power. (I consider the process theologies, by the way, as simply another very subtle variation on this theme.)[3] I still believe that my suggestions there are among the only tolerable and viable ways forward for faith and theology faced with the magnitude of evil. It is just that such alternatives have limitations and problems of their own which have propelled me hesitantly beyond them. When I came to write my 1975 study of Camus,[4] for the most part I simply shared in his heartache over human suffering and reaffirmed my rejection of a love that is omnipotent. I had very little to offer in the way of positive theological suggestions.

It is largely these human bondages of ours-- although there are other important reasons as well-- that have fundamentally altered my relationship to the languages and perspectives of the Bible and Christianity. Certain aspects of that tradition remain vibrantly meaningful as psychological, ethical, social, and historical insight, expressed often in such irreplaceably poetic and mythical form. The biblical and classical Christian perceptions of the creaturely slavery and the elusive possibilities of the self in all their ambiguous interpenetration and of the social implications of such selfhood continue to be the most adequate I know, as articulated so [5]masterfully in the writings of a Reinhold Niebuhr.[5] Developing those themes, the Augustinian theologians' insights into our utter creatureliness within an infinite and darkly mysterious scheme of things and the radical character of our tragic bondage provide an indispensable ontological framework for my reflections in the essays that follow. And long before Sam Keen told me in Beginnings Without End, I was quite consciously aware from my own life experience that death and resurrection--renewal through disintegration, finding oneself only through losing oneself--were built into the very structure of human life. I remain committed to a maximalized vision of the ethics of agape as the most creative and all-embracing direction the good life should take. And I continue to observe that the course of human history is truly unpredictable, full of suprises. These dimensions are the vital foci of my ongoing relationship to Christian theology, and of my continuing identification with the profound and distinctive caring for people and the world that I see in the Christian community at its best.

What is missing now from my relationship to Scripture and the Christian tradition is just that crucial foundational dimension of transcendence. Recognizing that it is precisely the believing encounter with the God of Israel and its interpretation out of which the insights I cherish come, I find nonetheless that it is this very God with whom I am no longer able to reckon. The living God has died for me partly because the bands of suffering with which the world is bound have squeezed God's reality first into a conundrum and then into an emptiness.

I hasten to add that I am not so naive as to think that the demise of the transcendent God within my own interpreted experience entails the

4

universalized conclusion that God does not exist. I have become increasingly impressed by the inescapably contextual character of all our "ultimate concerns." I can appreciate the fact that all sorts of people--some of whom I know and admire very much--deal with existence in terms of faith in the sovereign god of Abraham, Isaac, and Jacob. On questions of ultimate meaning absolutely none of us knows for sure who is closer to the mark. It is just that in my own ongoing struggle to make sense out of the Christian context of life- and world-interpretation, I find basic elements of that context which I simply cannot render coherent any longer.

Some time ago I had occasion to re-read one of my all-time favorite novels, Peter De Vries's 1961 book The Blood of the Lamb, in preparation for a course I was teaching on philosophical issues in modern fiction. The experience of going carefully back through the text brought into clarity and focus my groping realization of the death of God. The Blood of the Lamb is De Vries's most nearly autobiographical novel--and the most explicitly tragic effort of a writer best known for his hilarious albeit deeply compassionate commentary on contemporary American life. Like the author, the narrator-protagonist Don Wanderhope (whose surname, like others in De Vries's novels, is quite intentionally significant) grows up in a Dutch immigrant community in Chicago for whom vigorous, heady discussion of Calvinist theology is social meat and drink. Don's father Ben vacillates continually between faith and doubt; his adored older brother Louie, a medical student, is an outright and mocking skeptic. Don learns from both but ends up his father's son: unable to believe but unable to be a confident or comfortable unbeliever.

The all-pervading issue that hounds Don Wanderhope beyond both trusting faith and hard-nosed agnosticism is the deaths of those he loves. By the age of thirty-five or so he has experienced a succession of untimely deaths: his brother Louie at the age of twenty; Rena Baker, a fellow patient he falls in love with in a TB sanitarium; his wife Greta, who commits suicide after much inner torment. Finally Don suffers the slow dying of his only child

5

Carol at age eleven, as De Vries himself lost his
only daughter Emily, of leukemia. The most precious
thing in Don's life--all he has left of all those
who are dear to him--Carol is the "lamb" through
whose diseased blood he climactically experiences
the only grace, the only redemption he can finally
understand.

Having rejected the Dutch Reformed Calvinism of
his childhood, whose all-controlling God he is
unable to distinguish morally from the Devil, the
adult Don Wanderhope continues somewhat
spasmodically to seek some glimpse of ultimate
meaning amid the personal tragedies of his otherwise affluent Connecticut commuter life. His
ambivalent search reaches a certain peak of
intensity during the last days of Carol's life. He
is compellingly absorbed in the Christ figure on a
big crucifix over the entrance to a Catholic church
he passes frequently across the street from the
hospital. One of the most significant and memorable
scenes in the novel occurs when Don, having gotten
very drunk after Carol dies, throws a birthday cake
intended for her and hits in the face the crucified
Christ over the church entrance.

It was miracle enough that the pastry
should reach its target at all, at that
height from the sidewalk. The more so that
it should land squarely, just beneath the
crown of thorns. Then through scalded eyes
I seemed to see the hands free themselves of
the nails and move slowly toward the soiled
face. Very slowly, very deliberately, with
infinite patience, the icing was wiped from
the eyes and flung away. I could see it
fall in clumps to the porch steps. Then the
cheeks were wiped down with the same sense
of grave and gentle ritual, with all the
kind sobriety of one whose voice could be
heard saying, "Suffer the little children to
come unto me. . . for of such is the kingdom
of heaven."(170)

For awhile after Carol's death Don carries a
small crucifix in his pocket. Like some other
skeptics in other times and places with a despairing
"will to believe," Don is reduced to clinging

6

tentatively but desperately to that tortured man on the cross as the one fragile glimpse of transcendence left in a world full of gaping wounds.

But the anguished and fragmentary vision of the God who is supremely revealed in the suffering and dying Jesus is a vision the logic of which Don's own experience cannot sustain. It demands instead another logical sort of development: from the dying man on the cross many centuries ago to the much more intensely real and tangible child dying on the hospital bed with the marks of medically-induced stigmata on her frail body.

> The Western Gate is closed. That exit
> is barred. One angel guards it, whose sword
> is a gold head smiling into the sun in a
> hundred snapshots. The child on the brink
> of whose grave I tried to recover the faith
> lost on the edge of my brother's is the
> goalkeeper past whom I can now never get.
> In the smile are sealed my orders for the
> day. (174)

Don does not deny the existence of God. He simply cannot make any ultimate sense out of the deaths of a brother, a lover, a wife, above all a child, despite his anguished cries and "Whys?" to heaven. "'Let there be light,' we cry, and only the dawn breaks." (173)

By the end of the novel Don has flung the crucifix over the hedge. He settles for an even more modest doctrine:

> Now through the meadows of my mind wander
> hand in hand Louie and Carol. . . saying,
> 'My grace is sufficient for thee.' For we
> are indeed saved by grace in the end--but to
> give, not take. This, it seems then, is my
> Book of the Dead. All I know I have learned
> from them--my long-suffering mother and my
> crazy father, too, and from Greta. . . . All
> I am worth I got from them. And Rena too. .
> . . (174)

In Don's case it is his uniquely personal sharing in our common human encounter with the tragic

7

dimensions of death--participating in the suffering and dying of those we love, experiencing inconsolable grief--which grants and teaches him all he dares ask: the grace to care in turn for his fellow wayfarers in this vale of struggle and perplexity. "Time heals nothing--which should make us the better able to minister. There may be griefs beyond the reach of solace, but none worthy of the name that does not set free the springs of sympathy." (175)

With his tragicomic vision of the absurdities of the human condition, De Vries portrays with warmth and pathos a universal aspect of that condition in The Blood of the Lamb. As a son, a lover, a spouse, and a parent, I can emphathize keenly with Don Wanderhope's loves and losses. I also know all too well both Don's will and his incapacity to believe. In this connection De Vries's novel was a kind of parable bringing to full awakening my own hesitant realization of the death of God.

The God of classical faith and theology--the sovereign Creator, Preserver, and Consummator of absolutely everything who is nevertheless said personally to love his creatures--died for me some time ago, as I recorded in Borderland Christianity. Contemplation of the excessive estrangement and conflict and destruction and pain and waste on the earth came increasingly to render the vision of omnipotent love intolerably paradoxical and finally awful. As the young Don Wanderhope sums up his boyhood impression of his community's Calvinist faith: "Believe in God and don't put anything past him." (22)

At the same time, it is very important to emphasize that the vision of divine all-powerfulness possesses compelling logical and religious power, a power by which I have been and continue to be profoundly grasped. Given theism, it is legitimate to ask whether there can finally be a fully satisfying intellectual and spiritual apprehension of reality short of the infinity and all-embracing power of the Supreme Reality. And if God is such a reality, one may question the divine ways, cry out to and against God, and reject God, but one cannot finally escape God in life or in death. This vision

8

of deity has been for many Christians throughout the
centuries a foundational source of consolation and
hope, and for some a perception surely mystical in
its intensity and fullness. In this latter category
are Augustine and the great figures in the
Augustinian tradition such as Luther, Calvin, and
Edwards. Their doxological passion for the
plenitude and power of God is intimately and
dialectically related to their searingly
contemporary depth of insight into human
creatureliness and bondage. The vision of divine
omnipotence is not only terrible but also alluring,
not only dark but also profound. It is experience
of the holy as _mysterium_ _tremendum_ _et_ _fascinans_ in
the highest degree.

In the last analysis, however, the moral
objections arising from our human bondage to
compulsions from within and calamities from without
rise up like the painful lump in the throat before
weeping, choking off whatever "Hallelujahs" I may at
times be inclined to voice. In his modern rendering
of the story of Job, _J. B._, Archibald MacLeish
could not finally stare the vision of almightiness
in the face. God, J.B. concludes, does not love;
God simply is. Only we can love, and for all its
frailty and ambiguity that love is all we have. J.
B. and his wife Sarah join in saying, "The coal of
the heart. . . It's all the light now."[8] Even if
God is and is finally inescapable, there are those
for whom integrity and outrage and human empathy
demand rejecting, defying, or ignoring such a
reality.

Christian theologies "after Auschwitz" have
experienced the full anguish of the problem of Job.
There is far more reticence about the meaning of
God's almightiness and a theological silence in the
face of human suffering that simply shares
compassionately with those who undergo it and takes
action to alleviate it. Yet contemporary theologies
(including my own previous reflections in _Borderland
Christianity_) have remained trapped in the classic
dilemma which I shall express by paraphrasing
Augustine's formulation of it: Either God is
omnipotent but, in view of the state of the world
and human life, not good; or God is good but not
finally in sovereign control of the course of the

9

world, a being struggling in some sense as we are. The latter alternative has been understandably appealing, but both theologically and religiously it is not without serious deficiencies in view of the actual extent and power of the bondage "built into" human life and its environment.

I continue to regard theological struggles to interpret God as in some way finite $_9$to be lively options and worthy of the effort.^{9} Yet what has happened in my own case is that I have reluctantly discovered that for me this attempt to preserve a transcendence conceived as personal and purposive may have been only a temporary remission, not a cure. For a God who is less than ultimate power may be morally admirable, but compared to the superabundant power of our earthly bondages such a God appears somewhat impotent and seems to operate very raggedly. The older picture of an inscrutable Absolute in whose hands we can nevertheless at least be sure we are held for good or ill, whether in life or in death, has given way to the modern **Bild** of a kind of sympathetically groping, eagerly persuasive deity who does the best it can with all sorts of obstacles in a way beyond its control. The Dutch Calvinist God of Don Wanderhope's people may have behaved like the very devil, but at least that God was inescapable and held all the cards; the outcome was not in doubt. The Taolike God of an up-for-grabs universe who rolls with the punches manages to look a little too defeated to me, while God's many adversaries remain full of fight. I am at last impaled on the horns of Augustine's old dilemma, pithily expressed by Nickles's repeated jingle in **J.B.**:

> I heard upon his dry dung heap
> That man cry out who cannot sleep:
> "If God is God He is not good,
> If God is good He is not God;
> Take the even, take the odd. . . ."^{10}

In relation to the problem of human bondage and anguish the idea of the "death of God" may signify one of two things: (1) the inability to affirm a transcendent God of either infinite or finite power; or (2) some positive use or other of the radical theological interpretation of Christ as the complete

10

self-emptying of God into human life and the world.
Most problem-of-evil skeptics of course affirm the
death of God in sense (1) but not in sense (2). I
have been relating how God has also "died" for me in
this first sense. But as a skeptic who continues to
relate himself to insights embodied in the Christian
tradition, I also want to affirm the continuing
existential value of the death of God as a
theological insight.

As I recollect it, the myth of the death of God
affirms that the meaning of the incarnation,
supremely of the cross of Christ, is that the
sovereign transcendent Creator empties him/herself
wholly into the creation. God "dies" completely to
her/his transcendent status and identifies entirely
with humankind and our world.The only revelation of
God is the faces of us unlikely human beings, God's
only worship our compassionate devotion to one
another and to the needs of our earth. I must
confess that this version of the Christian myth is
the one I now find personally tolerable and
meaningful. Is it biblical? Of course not--but
both historically and at the present time none of
the many varieties of Christian faith and theology
are "biblical" but various sorts of imaginative
development and more or less logical implication out
of the biblical sources. How seriously do I take
it? As seriously as I take my continued involvement
with Christian theology--and as lightly and
irreverently as a Zen master takes the myths of the
Buddha relative to his pursuit of enlightenment. I
must also emphasize that I do not interpret the
death of God as a cosmic and historical event, as
Thomas Altizer did, but as a poetic or metaphorical
way of existentially rendering and appropriating a
compassionate humanism.

The death of God myth symbolically articulates,
from within the Christian perspective which is my
religious framework as well as Don Wanderhope's, my
own inability any longer to go beyond him--to affirm
anything more in the way of grace and love than the
human faces and voices and bodies around me, those
persons with whom I enter into relationships of
various kinds and intensities and patterns of
communion and brokenness. They are all so fallible
and fragile like me, but they are all I have for

11

sure. Luther's well-known words have become
undialectically true: "One shall be Christ to
another." I am becoming reluctantly content, in the
words of Camus, to "live with what I know."

Nor, like Camus, can I overlook the earth
itself. What graces it too bestows together with
its afflictions! That young redbud tree delicately
budding in my front yard in early spring, that
golden haze in which the rolling hills close to my
home are bathed on a summer morning, that lovely
pond on my walk home from work out of whose rushes a
redwinged blackbird almost invariably flies up as I
pass by in early autumn, that winter belt of trees
across the street transformed by an ice storm into a
glittering fairyland--all those beauties of which
nature is so achingly and serendipitously full are
likewise my modest sources of healing and renewal.
These human and natural graces must be sufficient
for me. I am slowly, painfully becoming resigned to
learning from them how to live, how to love, and, I
hope, how to die.

Have I suffered the tragic deaths of persons
close to me, like Don Wanderhope? Not at all.   I
said that the untimely deaths of those he loved were
his chief stone of stumbling. Other stumblers are
burdened by the excessive absurdities and cruelties
of life in varying ways. I can identify with Don's
particular experiences, by reading his story and
realizing with a clammy sweat what it would do to me
to lose my wife or one of my daughters. But for me
it is anguished contemplation of the world around me
present and past, attentive involvement with and
observation of persons and situations, and repeated
self-examination that create a cumulative impression
of tragically disproportionate bondage. Some of the
specific stimuli of my sober reflections have been
the histories of the fiendishly diverse injustices,
cruelties, tyrannies and butcheries human beings
have inflicted on one another--in particular the
long, appalling story of Jewish suffering at the
hands of Christian Europe with its insane climax
under the Nazis; Camus's searing reflections on our
blood-soaked century; accounts of the horrors of
plagues and epidemics at whose complete mercy human
beings for so long existed; and insights of depth
psychology into the character and influence of the

12

unconscious, childhood and repression in our behavior.

My own life up to this point has been on balance remarkably pleasant and favored. However, I attribute such good fortune to a lucky combination of contingencies which many, many persons on this earth do not enjoy. To call such contingencies "blessings of God" too blatantly suggests to me a very capricious omnipotence or a finite deity who has managed to exert a bit of benevolent control in this particular instance--and either way I am back with my old problem.

Perhaps surprisingly, by no means is my recent experiencing of the death of God to be equated with an abandonment of the very possibility of transcendence. One of my cardinal beliefs of long standing which I see no reason to give up is a strong suspicion that the reality of both ourselves and the cosmic context in which we find ourselves is far richer than we know and doubtless contains dimensions of which we have only scratched the surface. Even in this sense transcendence may have all the depth and richness I at least could ask: mystery, ineffability, ecstasy, reunion and reconciliation, worlds upon worlds of various sorts and stages of existence, an ideal order of which our experiences of truth, beauty, and goodness are fragmentary glimpses.

My problem is that I can no longer make sense out of certain images of transcendence, and specifically the Christian image of the loving, personal Creator and Redeemer. Nor can I relate in any meaningful way at all my very general beliefs about transcendence to all the absurd and tragic things that go on in this little sphere of reality called earth. I simply cannot get the transcendent and the earthly together coherently--and so I content myself with what I know, with the earthly.

I am somewhat drawn to certain aspects of what I understand of the world orientation of Gotama the Buddha: the difficult art of learning to accept the quite specific limitations and possibilities of my life without making myself unhappy struggling to affirm beliefs I cannot honestly affirm. One of my

13

favorite sources of consolation is the Buddha's famous dialogue from the Pali canon on "Questions Not Tending to Edification." I am trying--haltingly and amateurishly--to incorporate some of his wisdom, but I am still more comfortable dealing with my life-situation largely in the more familiar terms of the Christian tradition. And at this stage in my pilgrimage that has come to mean two things, both arising from my anguished encounter with the problem of bondage and the loss of transcendence. One is the poetizing of my experience in terms of the myth of the God who in Christ dies to his/her deity and lives only as grand and miserable human beings within this beautiful spoiled Eden called earth. The other is a deepening exploration of human creatureliness and bondage and the meaning of grace on the basis of a demythologized Augustinian vision of life--an exploration which I conduct in the pages that follow.

14

FOOTNOTES

[1]Trans. by Stuart Gilbert, N.Y.: Modern Library, 1948, p. 197.

[2]Nashville: Abingdon Press, 1973, chs. III, IV, and V.

[3]Se, e.g., Schubert Ogden, "Evil and Belief in God: The Distinctive Relevance of a 'Process Theology.'" The Perkins School of Theology Journal, 31, 4 (Summer 1978), pp. 29-34. Professor Ogden's article is in part a response to the original version of this essay ("The Death of God: A Belated Personal Postscript," The Christian Century, vol. xcii, no. 43, Dec. 29, 1976, pp. 1175-1178).

[4]Camus: A Theological Perspective, Nashville: Abingdon Press, 1975.

[5]See esp. The Nature and Destiny of Man, N. Y.: Scribner's, 1949, Pt. I.

[6]N.Y.: Harper & Row, 1975.

[7]N.Y.: New American Library, 1961. References from this book will be noted with page numbers in parentheses.

[8]Cambridge: The Riverside Press, 1958, p. 153.

[9]Among recent works see, e.g., Howard R. Burkle, God, Suffering, and Belief, Nashville: Abingdon Press, 1977.

15

[10] P. 11.

[11] For the most dramatic and well-developed theological expression of these views, see Thomas Altizer, _The Gospel of Christian Atheism_: Phila.: Westminster, 1966.

"ESSENTIAL" CALVINISM AS CONTEMPORARY WISDOM

   Whereas the language of Calvinism is in
disrepute, the elements of good sense in
Calvinism must always remain wherever there
is good sense. Piety is not dead. So long
as men refuse to shut their eyes to the
world, so long as they recognize their
connection with and their dependence upon a
world which supports them and often ignores
their personal welfare, so long as they find
happiness in self-denial and a love which
grows out of wisdom, so long as their sense
of the tragedy of life persists and can be
transmuted into victory over the world,--
there will be the essence of Calvinism.

The late Joseph Haroutunian wrote these lines in
the "Prelude" to his classic study of the decline of
Edwardean Calvinism in New England, Piety Versus
Moralism.[1] Haroutunian's words have increasingly
come alive for me in the context of my own
ponderings. I have long believed that at its best
the Augustinian tradition, of which Calvinism is the
most fully developed and consistent expression,
enshrines the profoundest wisdom about the human
condition to be found in Christianity. Two central
elements of that tradition's wisdom stand out
familiarly but importantly: (1) an overwhelming
sense of the total dependence and interdependence of
human beings as creatures among myriad creatures;
and (2) a sober perception of the radical depth and
breadth of that human estrangement which makes of
our dependence a tragic bondage. Out of this vision
of reality came a disciplined style of life that was
directed away from self and toward responsibility
for the world, tried to exercise love on the basis
of a balanced realism about both our brokenness and
our possibilties, and believed that the only form of
happiness fully tailored to our world is a joy the
world cannot overcome.

What impresses me about Professor Haroutunian's statement is that he managed succinctly to demythologize and secularize the Calvinist vision and lifestyle in such a way as to exhibit its timeless and timely wisdom. It is a wisdom that is only confirmed and reinforced by twentieth-century developments in the natural and social sciences. Professor Haroutunian's distillation of a "non-theological" essence out of the Calvinist tradition has provided a kind of charter for a skeptical theologian like me to reclaim as a viable, late-twentieth-century "natural piety" the incomparably rich insights of the Augustinian heritage. In this essay I want to engage in some hermeneutical work on Professor Haroutunian's words, without of course wishing to claim that what I have found in them is any more than. . . what _I_ have found in them.

1. The Vision

I begin with two propositions derived from Professor Haroutunian's remarks that I believe ought to commend themselves to those who "refuse to shut their eyes to the world": (1) Human life is indeed profoundly connected with and dependent upon that natural environment which both "supports" us and "often ignores. . . [our] personal welfare." Twentieth-century scientific inquiry in physics, chemistry, and biology massively reinforces and enriches the picture of a uni-verse that is a unified web of total interdependence from electron to galaxy. Our complete human involvement in that web of interdependence is confronting us urgently and practically as we hover dangerously close to what may be a point of no return in our heedless exploitation of earth's ecosystem. At its best the so-called "conquest of nature" by technology consists of adapting our dependence upon it in new ways so as to gain a greater measure of control over our environment and our lives. At its worst it reflects a tragically destructive _hubris_ that attempts to deny our dependence.

The scientific picture of our interdependent relationship with our natural environment has also brought with it the recognition that that environment is in itself _indifferent_. It does indeed support us and sustain our lives in countless marvellous ways--which of course is not surprising since we are products of the evolutionary process and at least physiologically adapted to our natural context for survival. Beyond that, nature sustains us by delighting our spirits through our senses with myriad forms of unsurpassable beauty and by providing the raw material for the creation of the many facets of human culture. And yet of course in the working out of the evolutionary process according to what Jacques Monod calls the combined principles of "chance and necessity,"^{2} nature also indifferently throws up a multitude of things that decidedly "ignore our personal welfare" as human beings. The virus and the epidemic, the genetic roulette that produces birth defects and may play a large role in personality disorders, the tornado and the flood--these afflict us quite randomly and heedlessly. We have in recent times been able in part to understand their workings and mitigate their impact. But again, it has only been through facing up to and coping with our dependence that we have succeeded as well as we have. Significantly, it has been precisely the scientific assumption that human beings are to be studied as creatures of nature, subject at least in very large part to its laws and surviving only in complex interdependence with it, that has played a foundational role in this new adaptation.

My second proposition is as follows: (2) We human beings are irrevocably dependent upon nature not only externally but also internally, and unfortunately in neurotic ways. The enduring legacy of Freud's pioneering insights is the general recognition that our individual and corporate behavior is dominated by repressed desires and conflicts which are produced by the unique biological nature and early environmental situation of human beings. To be sure, the unconscious is the mysterious wellspring of our gods and goods--love, aspiration, creativity. But the demons hidden in those same depths are more than a match for these divinities, and even the latter are ultimately dependent upon forces we gratefully make use of but only partially understand. In both its personal and its social dimensions human life is at best a creative dependence, at worst a vicious bondage.

Our tragic destiny as a species and as individuals on the earth is that the bondage so often predominates, lying in wait like cancerous cells to destroy the fragile tissues of sanity, love, justice, beauty, knowledge, and hope or openly devouring them. As Calvin aptly wrote, "a veritable world of miseries is to be found in mankind."[3] What makes the present world situation and future prospects cause for uneasiness is not that we are any more compulsive than people have ever been, but that we have so much greater power to destroy. A hard and careful consideration of myself, the people and institutions around me, and the world of nations gives rise indeed to what Haroutunian calls a "sense of the tragedy of life."

The common theme of my two propositions is our thoroughgoing "connection with and . . . dependence upon" the world of which we are an integral part. It is a connection and dependence which, as I have said, is not only external but also internal, built into our very bone and psychic marrow. Both outer and inner nature are the fruitful condition of all the goods we know, but they are also the indifferent source of our infirmities and woes. External nature is both a womb and a wantonness. What we call moral evil, which we contrast with natural evil, is at least to a very large degree "natural" as well: the compulsive expression of psychic conflicts deeply rooted in our human nature and childhood which likewise "ignore our personal welfare." The combination of our profound dependencies upon both the outer and the inner world results in the intensity of the tragedies that we both suffer and inflict upon one another.

2. The Virtues

Thus the sobering indicative, the conviction of our utter creatureliness and bondage; what of the imperative, the implications for living that it yields? The "essential" Calvinism I am reading off Professor Haroutunian's statement replies in this way: It is precisely such a situation that calls forth, from those who are able by the grace of heredity and circumstances to respond, a disciplined and actively compassionate responsibility to transcend self-preoccupation and do what they can to alleviate human suffering and liberate human potentialities wherever and whenever possible. Such a lifestyle will always be marked by stumbling and halting, serious errors, and the other frustrations and failures born of inescapable participation in our creaturely bondages--but all this is only to say that it is a human calling, not an excuse for fatalism. For it will also be characterized by achievements and satisfactions, triumphs and beauties, solidarity and relationship.

a. Self-denial

Professor Haroutunian indicates that happiness, for persons called by their perception of the world to an "essential" Calvinism, arises from two virtues: "self-denial," and "a love which grows out of wisdom." In our day happiness is decidedly "in" and self-denial emphatically "out," and the notion that the latter can produce the former tends to be one of those quaint pieties to which we give solemn lip service but no existential allegiance. Many of us in the Western middle classes are dedicated to the intensely individual pursuit of happiness as self-fulfillment, seen as the contrary of self-denial. I am entitled to happiness, which I interpret in terms of freedom to "be my own person," to "find myself," to "discover my identity," to "realize my potentialities." In this pursuit of self-fulfillment as a kind of natural right--which also typically includes what I satisfiedly consider harmless forms of sensate indulgence--I am inclined to be impatient about quotidian restraints on my unfettered pursuit of happiness.

The contemporary quest for individual happiness as self-fulfillment is in part one very positive expression of a general and healthy liberating process in our time, one manifestation of the movement in all areas of life in industrialized societies on behalf of human dignity, diversity, and potentiality. But I think it will readily be granted that like all things human, the quest is ambivalent: it is also in part an excuse for selfishness and self-indulgence, for a hedonism that rationalizes withdrawal from the often hard demands

21

of interpersonal commitments and social responsibilities in the name of "freedom."

Now what I find very significant and often downright daunting is that human nature seems to be so constructed that the pursuit of happiness as pleasure or self-fulfillment is inherently self-defeating; it does not succeed. The structure of selfhood appears to be such that I cannot attain the goal of happiness by making it my goal. Self-satisfaction and self-realization are, perhaps paradoxically, byproducts of orientation away from the self toward goals outside the self--that is, in the world.

The Viennese psychotherapist Viktor Frankl is among those who have articulated this analysis of human behavior on the basis of clinical experience and phenomenological description of consciousness. According to Frankl, the inherent structure of human awareness is intentionality; that is, consciousness by its very nature "tends" or is directed away from itself toward objects outside itself. Thus the dynamic of the human self is essentially a self-transcending, an orientation beyond itself to the world around it. To put it in the terms of one of Jesus' more profound psychological insights, the self "finds" itself precisely by "losing" itself in response to its environment, an environment made up of tasks to perform, knowledge to acquire, other persons to enter into relationships with and at the very least to reckon with, and things and goals regarded as worthy of pursuit. Frankl subsumes the whole of this human self-transcending or tending toward the world under the concept of the "will to meaning" as the primary motivational force in human beings. The will to meaning is the human striving for reasons and purposes in life, which we characteristically fulfill through responding to these realities other than ourselves: deeds, objects of knowledge, other persons, valued things and ideals.[4]

On this view the pursuit of pleasure or self-actualization as ends in themselves is inherently self-defeating because of the structural orientation of the self away from itself toward the world. Pleasure and self-fulfillment are effects of

22

realizing meaningful goals outside the self. As Frankl writes, "Attaining the goal constitutes a reason for being happy. . . . if there is a reason for happiness, happiness ensues, automatically and spontaneously, as it were." Of self-actualization he remarks, "Only to the extent to which man fulfills a meaning out there in the world, does he fulfill himself. . . . self-actualization is the unintentional effect of life's intentionality."[6] The quest for pleasure or self-realization as ends in themselves results from the frustration of the will to meaning and attempts to compensate for it. What Frankl tries to show both his clients and his readers is that the effort is doomed to frustration and failure because of the very character of the human self in its interaction with the world.

It is by no means necessary to agree with all of Frankl's terminology or psychological analysis (I certainly do not) in order to recognize here an important insight confirmed in our experience: Searching for happiness or self-fulfillment is a will-o-the-wisp. I realize meaningful goals such as sharing in the healing of a close relationship with another person, working together with others to enrich the community or alleviate the deprivation of some of its members in some small way, solving a challenging problem, doing a household project, teaching, playing a Chopin etude, writing these lines. The actualizing of these varied purposes in the world outside myself inherently produces satisfaction, happiness, fulfillment--usually of course without my even reflecting on it.

If such are the dynamics of selfhood, finding "happiness in self-denial" is not a pious irrelevance but an embodiment of an accurate perception of those dynamics. But the word "denial" linked with "self" sticks in the contemporary craw. We are all too familiar with the unhealthy behaviors that have passed themselves off and justified themselves as "self-denial": masochism, self-rightousness, various sorts of repression, a constipated joylessness and humorlessness. Calvinist piety strongly affirmed the necessity for self-denial, but doubtless in practice its self-denial too often took just these forms of self-deception.

All right, then; let us use Dr. Frankl's term and speak more positively and broadly of a reflective form of self-transcending--a conscious and thoughtful commitment to meaningful goals in the world outside the self.

But "reflective self-transcending" by itself does not say enough. It is necessary to fill it out with some of the "hard" content that the term "self-denial" points to, however inadequately. It is simply a fact, of which your experience and mine veritably shout their confirmation, that committing ourselves to the fulfilling of meanings in the world inevitably demands--what other word can I use?--some measure of self-denial! For the sake of those persons and things and ideals I truly value I am continually involved at least to some degree in saying "No" to--in denying (not of course in the sense of repressing but of consciously suppressing)--some of my own desires and needs. An obvious and common example of this is a close relationship with another human being, where mutual compromise and sacrifice for the sake of a larger, shared good are simply daily realities. But all areas of reflective self-transcending involve self-denial: consider the artist's dedication to her or his art, the exercise of public responsibility, caring for children, working at a job, the pursuit of knowledge.

The habit of character necessary to develop in order to sustain the self-denial demanded by reflective self-transcending is of course self-discipline. Our Calvinist forebears in Europe and the United States knew that well and valued it highly--indeed excessively. They also knew that, like all virtues and arts, self-discipline or self-control requires training over a period of time; conscious conditioning, as we might put it nowadays. Self-discipline is the self's habitual exercise of reasoned control over its impulses and wants for the sake of various ends. One central element in it is what we call the capacity for "deferred" or "long-range" gratifications. Self-discipline is always a very imperfect and unfinished process, and there are many persons whose "nature and nurture" effectively prevent them from achieving anything more than the most minimal self-discipline needed for their

24

survival. But necessary to survival self-discipline certainly is, for both individuals and societies; and necessary not only to survival but also to the realization of all the values that make human life humane and endurable. In one of his "notorious" (and compassionately reasoned) essays on marriage, Bertrand Russell put it succinctly: "The good life cannot be lived without self-control."[7]

Like pursuing the happiness of pleasure or self-fulfillment, trying to live without self-discipline and self-denial shatters itself on the brick wall of reality: we and the world we live in are simply not constructed in such a way as to make the attempt anything but an unhappy failure. My own self is so structured as to be oriented toward fulfilling meanings outside myself in the world; and that world is made up of other persons, of objects and forces and events, that exist and impose their presence upon me regardless of whether I "like" it or not. I am a totally interdependent creature, and interdependence at the human level depends among other things upon self-control and self-sacrifice.

But this perception is so damnably hard for you and me really to appropriate in any more than a halting and fitful way because of our personal and social bondages to forces within us over which we can exercise only partial control. Of course in this discussion I am attempting to describe healthy as opposed to unhealthy forms of self-discipline and -denial, while recognizing that mental "health" is always a relative notion. As we can see clearly in the case of self-control and self-sacrifice, it is also an achievement that extracts its price in terms of unconscious renunciation. The forms of self-discipline and self-denial I have in mind are those that are compatible with individuality and autonomy, self-respect and self-expression, critical self-awareness, spontaneity and creativity, flexibility, and intense feeling. But of course within the spectrum of mental "health" the inner relationship between these dimensions of personality and the demands of self-control may range from controlled conflict through creative tension to a more or less harmonious integration.

25

An old saying passed along to me by my father earthily expresses what I think many of us experience in this never-ending struggle with ourselves to "grow up" to the demands of reality: "We grow so soon old and so late smart"--to which I must add "if at all." And yet it is along the path of reflective self-transcending, containing as it inevitably does self-denial and self-discipline, that our "fitting" relationship to reality (that is, the one that fits) and thereby our authentic happiness are to be found--"or not at all."

b. Love

The other virtue of an "essential" Calvinism is "a love which grows out of wisdom." The wisdom that produces love is of course that twofold perception of reality that I described at the beginning of this essay: the soberly realistic vision of our utter creatureliness and our tragic bondage. As wisdom rather than merely knowledge, the vision is intensely existential as well as rational; it penetrates to the "heart and reins," sensitizing the whole person and not simply engaging the mind. The wisdom that Professor Haroutunian called the "essence of Calvinism" is more than reasoned awareness of our complete interdependence within the universe, although it is certainly that; it is also something like what Rudolf Otto called the "feeling of creatureliness,"[8] my realization of our common dependence "in my bones," as it were. That wisdom is similarly an honest and hard-eyed perception of the bonds that grip myself and others with the cords of compulsion and self-delusion; but it is also a perception that suffers acutely something of the concrete pains of that bondage.

And just here do we touch upon the positive ethics yielded up by a tragic wisdom. What else can such an ethics be but an ethics in which compassion is a central element? Com-passion: feeling or suffering together with a fellow being. This existential identification and solidarity with other human beings in their helplessness, deprivation, frustration, pain, and anguish seems to me to grow in a way naturally and compellingly out of what I have been calling an "essential Calvinism" or contemporary "natural piety."

26

Especially at this point I want to draw
attention to the fact that I am by no means claiming
that the specific views evoked for me by Professor
Haroutunian's modern distillation of the Calvinist
"essence" are materially those of traditional
Calvinism. The Calvinist tradition, for example,
attempted to stay within the boundaries of a
thoroughgoing biblical ethics. In keeping with
Professor Haroutunian's "universalizing" of elements
in that tradition and with the general method I have
adopted in this essay, I am dealing with ethical
emplications in wider albeit biblically-informed
terms.

It is vital to stipulate that a fully ethical
compassion is an active compassion. As I noted
earlier in this essay, it is precisely a world in
creaturely bondage that demands of those who are
able to respond compassionate activity to alleviate
concrete ills in whatever small and large ways they
can. Admittedly this is not the only possible
outcome of the tragic vision of life I have been
sketching. It may yield an acute sensitivity to the
suffering around one and in oneself that for various
reasons is overwhelmed and paralyzed into a passive
fatalism or a self-protective bitterness and
cynicism. I simply want to indicate that of the
possible implications of an "essential" Calvinism,
only an active compassion to alleviate suffering is
a properly ethical one.

The ethics arising from a tragic wisdom is
marked by realism in its decision-making, acting,
and evaluating. It seeks on the one hand seriously
to take into account the depths of the personal and
social bondages that determine our behavior, often
in destructive and demonic ways. It seeks on the
other hand always to elicit, actualize, and nurture
those mysteriously creative possibilities that also
characterize our individual and corporate human
condition. Achieving the balance demanded by such
an ethical realism is exceedingly difficult. Its
chief temptation is a despairing resignation, its
major impediment our imprisonment in our own
character patterns and social pathologies. The
achievement, needless to say, is always a fragile
and ambiguous one. Yet the obligation to make the
effort, however stumblingly, will not leave in peace

27

those who "refuse to shut their eyes to the world"--those who cannot avert their eyes from the need and pain around and within them crying out for succor and hope.

Such a love is clearly a manifestation of what I have called reflective self-transcending. Indeed, according to the Christian tradition a love ensouled by active compassion--or something very like it--is the highest expression of that self-transcending. It is clearly an orienting of the self away from itself toward the world: a compelling albeit painful reaching out to the world of other selves bound together with me in creaturely bondage.

Just as obviously does this form of reflective self-transcending involve self-discipline and self-denial. I simply cannot fulfill the obligations arising from identification and solidarity with the human beings around me without some deliberate suppression of my own needs and desires. Commitment to a close relationship with another person or other persons demands constant adjustments, compromises, and sacrifices on matters ranging from everyday decisions to struging and sharing over the very nature of the relationship. Serious response to the many and urgent voices of deprivation and suffering all around me may require of me a commitment of time, energy, resources, and self that I would much rather expend elsewhere. And of course the capacity for such sacrifices is normally made possible on a sustained and mature basis in part by the cultivation of self-discipline, by a habitual governance of my own impulses and wants that at its best strengthens the self in responding regularly to the demands of active compassion.

But in those who involve themselves, however imperfectly and fitfully, in that self-transcending called love it can produce one of the most deeply satisfying forms of personal happiness. Perhaps it is the case that in this most daunting and inescapable sphere of self-transcending we experience a happiness whose intensity is directly proportional to the sheer difficulty of our hard-won and always temporary achievements. Perhaps, more profoundly, our satisfaction results from an intuitive sense that authentic union of person with

28

person, sharing of persons in community and
liberation of persons by persons from some of their
bondage into at least a modicum of human dignity and
well-being, are somehow a touching down upon "what
it's really all about," a momentary participation in
what is in some sense "most real."

3. The Victory

But now we come to the final characteristic of
the "essential" Calvinism sketched by Professor
Haroutunian: the persistence of a "sense of the
tragedy of life" that "can be transmuted into
victory over the world" (my italics). "Ay, there's
the rub." Here, it seems, we are abruptly brought
up short in our attempt to secularize and
demythologize the Calvinist tradition into a
contemporary wisdom. The sober perception of our
creaturely dependence and human bondage, the virtues
of self-denial and active compassion as essential to
a style of life tailored to the realities of self
and world--these we can, I think, accept and
appropriate as modern "worldly" persons. But
"victory over the world"? That appears impossible
apart from the theistic faith that some of us find
problematic.

The assurance of victory over the world was
rooted for traditional Calvinism in an unshakeable
confidence in the absolute sovereignty of the
infinite and eternal God over the created order, as
a whole and in the minutest detail. Calvin's
statement in his Geneva Catechism of 1546 is
succinctly representative:

. . . as the world was once made by God, so
it is now preserved by him, and. . . the
earth and all other things endure just in so
far as they are sustained by his energy, and
as it were his hand. Besides, seeing that
he has all things under his hand, it
follows, that he is the chief ruler and Lord
of all. Therefore, by his being "creator of
heaven and earth," we must understand that
it is he alone who by wisdom, goodness, and
power, guides the whole course and order of
nature: who at once sends rain and drought,

29

hail and other storms, as well as calm, who
of his kindness fertilizes the earth, and on
the contrary, by withholding his hand, makes
it barren: from whom come health and
disease; to whose power all things are
subject, and whose nod they obey.⁹"

This same omnipotent Creator is of course also the
one who has decisively displayed the divine power
among human beings in Christ's victory over sin and
death by his death and resurrection from the dead.

By faith the believer knew that nothing befell
her or him without the will of the sovereign God
whose unfathomable wisdom ordered all things for the
divine glory. By faith the believer participated in
the risen life of Christ, really albeit partially
during this mortal life and fully in the life to
come. This twin confidence was, for those who
concretely appropriated it, a powerful source of
inner peace and joy and victory in a world filled
with danger, uncertainty, and suffering.

Nature with its seemingly arbitrary cruelty as
well as its nurture and beauty was in its every
operation the manifestation of the divine will that
transcended and controlled it; it was, as Jonathan
Edwards saw it, a kind of "language" of God in the
Creator's manifold speech to the creature. Our
helpless bondage resulted from Adam's fall and
Satan's thrall, which were themselves inscrutably
permitted and circumscribed by the all-powerful Lord
and overcome by God's utterly free and undeserved
grace bestowed in Christ on the elect "chosen from
the foundation of the world." All things whatsoever
in the universe--past, present, and to come--were
totally embraced within the reality and infallibly
directed by the unsearchable wisdom of the sovereign
Being who infinitely transcended them.

But what basis does a contemporary, secularized
distillation of Calvinist wisdom possibly have for
transmuting its "sense of the tragedy of life" into
"victory over the world"? Is it not restricted to
being what we usually think of as a modern
stoicism--a tragic vision of human life and the
world without hope of transcendence and redemption,
combined with a strong commitment to doing what one

30

can to alleviate human suffering while there is time? On this view there would seem to be no victories over the world, but only never-ending bandagings of the world's wounds and the always-threatened establishing of temporary sectors of health within the world.

It is common to refer to some of the great humanists of this century as "modern stoics." For our purposes I shall mention only Bertrand Russell and Albert Camus. Each in his own way seems admirably to exemplify the characteristics of what I have been describing as an "essential" Calvinism—except apparently for any sense of being able to transmute his tragic vision of reality into "victory over the world." Both were profoundly gripped by the silent indifference and relentless inexorability of nature, and by our dependent and precarious situation as its creatures. Both were existentially appalled—at times overcome—by the seemingly inexhaustible manifestations of human oppression and pain. Both were accustomed to the most committed sort of self-denial and self-discipline in their work, and affirmed that the most enduring and fulfilling human goods were not possible without such renunciation. Both responded with active compassion in the public arena to some of the urgent human needs of their time, speaking out vigorously on behalf of the victims of deprivation, denial of human rights, and the cruelty of war. Both believed that all our achievements were partial, ambiguous, and perishable, and on the basis of their experience of the world neither man could affirm a transcendent reality that would bestow ultimate significance and durability on those achievements. Indeed, in the light of their acute perceptions of the tyranny of external nature and the agony of human nature Russell regarded the traditional Christian affirmations of both the omnipotence and the goodness of God as simply monstrous, morally obscene; Camus, a bit more sympathetically, appreciated something of both the existential force and the existential anguish of the affirmations, but found them an insuperable stumbling block and a baneful influence on Western history.

Thus two "modern stoics," two men of high intelligence, moral courage, and humane sensitivity

31

who soberly accepted the challenges and shouldered the burdens of life amid the wreckage of a world whose God is dead or silent. No experience of "victory over the world" here --or is there? Listen to Russell--who like Camus won the Nobel Prize for Literature--at the beginning of his autobiography, written in his later years. In the Dedication, "To Edith," he writes:

> Now, old and near my end
>   I have known you,
> And, knowing you,
>   I have found both ecstasy and peace.
>   I know rest.
> After so many lonely years,
>   I know what life and love may be.
> Now, if I sleep,
>   I shall sleep fulfilled.[10]

Russell entitled the Prologue to his autobiography "What I Have Lived For." There he describes the "three passions" that have governed his life: a need for love, a thirst for knowledge, and an almost unendurable pity for humankind in its bondage and pain. It is the section on love that belongs together with the lines I have quoted from the dedication, and it contains these extraordinary words:

> I have sought love, first, because it brings ecstasy--ecstasy so great that I would often have sacrificed all the rest of life for a few hours of this joy. I have sought it, next, because it relieves loneliness--that terrible loneliness in which one shivering consciousness looks over the rim of the world into the cold unfathomable lifeless abyss. I have sought it, finally, because in the union of love I have seen, in a mystic miniature, the prefiguring vision of the heaven that saints and poets have imagined. This is what I sought, and though it might seem too good for human life, this is what--at last--I have found.[11]

Camus's life and thought had as their living center the expansive beauty of the sun-drenched

North African coast on which he grew up. As a young man he experienced the ecstasy of near-mystical union with the concrete sights and smells of his Algerian environment, and described such experiences as his "nuptials with the world" in his early book of essasys called Nuptials. It was the sun--dominating, radiating, nurturing, searing--that became for him symbolic of that world, and also of the light of clarity and truth that he admired in the ancient Greeks and prized in his own writing and commitments.

One of Camus's favorite places as a young man was Tipasa, with its Roman ruins mingled together with wildflowers; he described his intoxicating union with the area in "Nuptials at Tipasa," written in 1936. Years later, having survived the horrors of the Second World War as a member of the French resistance and now witnessing the grim drama of the Cold War unfold, he went back to Tipasa. It was for Camus a restoration and renewal at the wellsprings of his life and a realization of what had secretly sustained him through all those bitter years. He describes it in the powerful and moving essay "Return to Tipasa":

. . . I discovered one must keep a freshness and a source of joy intact within, loving the daylight that injustice leaves unscathed, and returning to the fray with this light as a trophy. Here, once more, I found an ancient beauty, a young sky, and measured my good fortune as I realized at last that in the worst years of our madness the memory of this sky had never left me. It was this that in the end saved me from despair. I had always known that the ruins of Tipasa were younger than our drydocks or our debris. In Tipasa, the world is born again each day in a light always new. Oh light! The cry of all the characters in classical tragedy who came face to face with their destinies. I knew now that their final refuge was also ours. In the depths of winter, I finally learned that within me there lay an invincible summer.[12]

33

For Russell the ecstasy and union of love with another human being, for Camus the ecstatic union with the sunlight-filled world of his childhood and youth: these were enduring inner possessions-- "kingdoms," Camus would have called them--which the world could not take away, supreme experiences of joy and peace and completeness, inexhaustible sources of strength and nourishment amid the difficult tasks to be done and the cries of pain to be heeded. These concrete ec-stasies (a "standing out from" or transcending of themselves) were experiences of self-transcending that moved uniquely beyond all other kinds of self-transcending for Russell and Camus by being an ever-renewable and - renewing inner "still point" above the strife. Is it utterly far-fetched of me to suggest that what all this adds up to is a kind of "victory over the world"? Not cosmic, not everlasting, but for all that real and worthy of the name?

Ontologically, of course, there are fundamental differences between Russell's and Camus's "victories" and the "victory" of the Christian believer. The transcendence that Russell and Camus believed they experienced was not the God who infinitely transcends and undergirds all things, but certain purely intra-mundane life-experiences that became for them lodestars amid their terrestrial searchings. The enduring quality of their ecstasies was a perishable permanence, they belived, that did not outlast the grave, not a proleptic participation in the divine eternity.

But I see no essential difference psychologically between the ways in which their ecstasies functioned for Russell and Camus and the ways in which an experiential faith functions for the believer. There are the common elements of grace, union, peace, bliss, joy, assurance, fulfillment, renewal, and--basic to it all-- rootedness in that which the world can neither overcome nor take away. As a matter of fact, one of the things that immediately strikes the reader about these and other testimonies of Russell and Camus to the supreme values in their life is their identifiably "religious" tone and even content. I suggest that the only truly relevant and adjudicable factor in all experiences of "victory over the world" is precisely their function in the lives of those who have and are guided by them. The profound love Russell had found with Edith was no less an experience of transcendence _for_ _him_ than is the earnest Christian's experience of what she or he believes to be God for her or him. And indeed, in view of the objective state of our ignorance regarding ultimate reality and life after death (for even the believer "walks by faith"), what significant criterion for "victory over the world" can there be other than the testimony of those "saints with and without God" as well as other believers and non-believers to their experiencing and in some way shaping their lives by various sorts of ecstasies?

Russell and Camus were able to transmute their tragic sense of life into a kind of victory over the world while fully believing that human life and all that was best in it--including the sources of their own ecstasies--were completely annihilated in death. Historically the term eternal has had three closely related but clearly distinguishable meanings: (1) the more traditional and fundamental application to a supreme reality that cannot not-exist, understood as either time-less--existing "outside" the temporal process altogether--or as embracing but transcending all temporality, as when God is described as eternal; (2) a derivative, somewhat looser sense of "eternal," to refer to an "unending," qualitatively transformed existence of human selves after death, as in the common usage of the expression "eternal life"; and (3) a certain cluster of qualities of present experience: "timeless" in the sense that time seems to stand still or melt into the background, transcendent in that it spontaneously takes the experiencer quite out of herself or himself and seems to inhabit a dimension of reality all its own, gracious in happening unbidden and unforced. Surely in this third and--at least in literature and chiefly in poetry--by no means uncommon sense Russell's and Camus's life-sustaining and life-orienting ecstasies were experiences of what is "eternal." As Ludwig Wittgenstein expressed it precisely in terms of the notion of "eternal life": "If we take eternity to mean not infinite temporal duration but timelessness then eternal life belongs to those who live in the present."[13]

All who have experienced wonder, union and communion, beauty, and discovery know something of participation in the eternity or timelessness of the "now." In my own life it has probably been beauty--chiefly in nature and in music--that has been the most powerful producer of "eternal presents." But of course in the context of my discussion of "victory over the world," I must ask myself whether any of my own ecstasies function specifically for me, as they did for Russell and Camus, as a unique self-transcending, an inner "still point" that enduringly elevates and sustains and fulfills me amid the bondage I see and feel all around me. That, it seems to me, is the test by which we must distinguish those momentary "peak-experiences" that many of us have but which do not focus and guide our lives from those that do provide such a permanent transcendent reference and hence a "victory over the world." In my own case I am simply not sure. On the one hand I have come to find moments of beauty--and also times of union with persons I love--increasingly precious as all I am likely to know of eternity and ever-renewed possessions that the ugliness and estrangement within and around me cannot stain. On the other hand my appropiation of these ecstasies is very fitful and liable to despair, and admixed with a lingering Platonic hope that they are not simply what they are but also shadowy revelations of an eternity that engulfs our temporality and overcomes our death. My own participation in the eternity of the present is certainly necessary to life and sanity; the question is, is it sufficient unto itself to "give me the victory"? I am not sure.

And yet I do not want to make too much of the difference between ecstasies that many just "have" and ecstasies that sustain the lives of some. It is a difference of degree, I believe, and not of kind--and that is also a consolation to me. Russell did not find the peace and fulfillment he had sought in love until late in his life. Camus realized his inner "summer" much earlier although not many years before his untimely death in a car accident. We know that both men experienced times when the unconquerable "sun" that illuminated their lives was eclipsed by deep depression and dissipated in its intensity by the cares that pressed upon them. Both men continued to falter and stumble, to doubt and waver. It is just that they found in their personal ecstasies, amid the cries of their fellows and the tasks to be done, a repeated and lasting source of victory that they recognized kept them going and gave the struggle meaning and value. There must be numerous approximations, conscious and partly-conscious, to such quietly ecstatic foci of meaning in the lives of others.

But not all others. We must bear in mind that there are also many persons who through severe deprivation--grinding poverty and labor, destructive oppression, loss of liberty and dignity, mental darkness or imprisonment--are largely cut off from ecstatic experiences and especially from the sort of unifying and overcoming ecstasies exemplified by Russell and Camus. The possibility of "victory over the world," like all other human possibilities, is contingent upon nature, nurture, circumstances, and within that context on whatever potentialities we have to cultivate openness to and integrate such experiences. Even those of us who must try to get along without God cannot get along without a doctrine of election and grace--albeit now the predestining of an indifferent "chance and necessity" rather than that of the inscrutable but purposive Lord.

That last remark reminds us of where all this began: with a contemporary vision of the world and a life-style that Professor Haroutunian called the "essence of Calvinism." Its foundational element is the unflinchingly honest awareness of our complete creaturely dependence and interdependence within the natural order and our tragic bondage to our own individual and corporate natures. Its chief virtues are three expressions of that self-transcending which is the dynamic orientation of our human existence: self-denial (with its enveloping presupposition self-discipline), the love that is informed by active compassion, and ecstasies that function for those who experience and are given anchor by them as "victory over the world."

To those for whom the transcendent God is dead it is in just these reflective forms of self-transcending that whatever divinity and transcendence they may glimpse is to be found. To those who recognize themselves in some way in this essay such a modest mysterium tremendum et fascinans may not be ultimately satisfying, but it must be sufficient for a life and is all they can affirm with integrity. Following Professor Haroutunian, I have called the vision and virtues I have sketched an "essential" Calvinism, because I continue to wrestle with contemporary issues in terms of their theological roots and relationships and find the Augustinian tradition singularly rich in its perspicacity about our creaturely bondage and its implications. That tradition, and especially the name "Calvinism," will be offputting to some readers. So be it; forget the label. I am (perhaps audaciously) content to think of what I have tried to describe--the virtues of which I am far from attaining--simply as "wisdom" or, in Professor Haroutunian's words, "good sense."

FOOTNOTES

[1] N.Y.: Harper Torchbooks, original copyright 1932, pp. xxxiixxxiii.

[2] *Chance and Necessity*, N.Y.: Random House, 1972.

[3] Calvin: *Institutes of the Christian Religion*. The Library of Christian Classics, ed. By John T. McNeill and trans. by Ford Lewis Battles, Philadelphia: Westminster Press, 1960, p. 36.

[4] A basic presentation of Frankl's theory appears in his classic *Man's Search for Meaning*, N.Y.: Washington Square, 1963, Part Two. See also his *The Doctor and the Soul*, N.Y.: Bantam Books, 1965; *Psychotherapy and Existentialism*, N.Y.: Simon and Schuster, 1967; and *The Will to Meaning*, N.Y.: New American Library, 1969.

[5] *The Will to Meaning*, p. 34.

[6] P. 38.

[7] *Marriage and Morals*, ch. 16. London: Allen & Unwin, 1957; reprinted in Raziel Abelson, ed., *Ethics and Metaethics: Readings in Ethical Philosophy*, N.Y.: St. Martin's Press, 1963, p. 91.

[8] *The Idea of the Holy*, trans by John W. Harvey, N.Y.: Oxford Univ. Press, 1958, pp. 8-11.

[9] From *John Calvin: Selections from His Writings*, ed. with an intro. by John Dillenberger,

Garden City: Doubleday Anchor Books, 1971, pp. 251-252.

[10] *The Autobiography of Bertrand Russell: 1872 to World War I,* N.Y.: Bantam Books, 1967.

[11] P. 3.

[12] *Lyrical and Critical Essays,* ed. & with notes by Philip Thody, trans. by Ellen Conroy Kennedy, N.Y.: Alfred A. Knopf, 1968, pp. 168-169.

[13] *Tractatus Logico-Philosophicus,* London: Routledge & Kegan Paul, 1961, 6.4311.

II.

OF HUMAN BONDAGE: AUGUSTINIANISM OLD AND NEW

The publication in 1971 of B. F. Skinner's
Beyond Freedom and Dignity [1] and the lively
controversy it aroused suggested that the freedom-
determinism issue is still very much with us. I
have been interested theologically in the scientific
determinism of twentieth-century secular thinkers
like Skinner and his quite different antecedent
Sigmund Freud as a kind of "secular Augustinianism"
in its world-outlook. Furthermore, as one who finds
the theoretical assumption of determinism
problematic but is very soberly impressed by the
empirical reality of our bondage, I have come to a
new appreciation of the profundity and relevance of
the Augustinian theological tradition. That
"determinism" is nowadays a theological taboo, that
contemporary Christians would be overwhelmingly
ranged against Skinner in the freedom-determinism
debate, reveals just how wide a gulf separates us
from the classical exemplars of that tradition--
Augustine, Luther, Calvin, and Edwards.

To be sure, there was the partial theological
hegemony earlier in this century of neo-orthodox
thinkers like Karl Barth and Reinhold Niebuhr, who
were deeply Augustinian in their outlook. But even
Barth with his triumphant sola gratia Calvinism, and
Niebuhr with his profound analysis of the deep-
seated ambiguities of the human self, were
acceptably "modern" theologians and therefore
modified Augustinians: both left some real scope
for human freedom. For all that, they have to a
significant degree been superseded by various forms
of neo-existentialism and process theology, with
their decidedly un-Augustinian emphasis on human
freedom.

So Augustinian determinism is apparently as dead
as a doornail within the theological circle. But
behold its revival in some of the most influential
secular thought of our era, psychoanalysis and
behaviorism: Causality is the sovereign controller

of all events and determiner of all destinies. Why causality determines all things in this way is finally an inscrutable mystery. But the causal process has made known to human beings, through scientific investigation, enough of its nature and operations to enable us to understand and modify our behavior and to change our environment as we desire. Through no merit of their own, but solely through the causal "grace" of heredity and environment, some human beings have had the eyes of their reason opened to discover, develop, learn, and utilize this scientific knowledge....All the elements of a secularized Augustinianism are here: total determination of all events, "grace," "saving" knowledge, election.

1. Determinist Perspectives, Philosophical and Theological

Some secular Augustinians are "soft" determinists, as were the old religious Augustinians. The soft determinist accepts universal causal explanation, but regards what she or he considers our ordinary usage of the concepts of freedom and responsibility as perfectly compatible with total causal determination; hence this version of the analysis of the problem of freedom is sometimes also called "compatibilism." Persons, on this view, are free insofar as their behavior is uncoerced or uncompelled. Coercion can be external, as for example when a person is forced by others to do something against her or his desires under threat of punishment or death; or it can be internal, as in cases of neurotic inner compulsions resulting from unconscious repression. The soft determinists thus interpret freedom behaviorally, as freedom of action, not freedom of will: it refers to my ability to put my own desires into effect without hindrance, to do what I will. When we say that a person "could have done otherwise" in a particular situation, the soft determinist says, what we mean by that is that she or he could have acted differently in different circumstances or with different desires. But of course our desires are expressions of our character, and character is the product of nature and nurture.

According to soft determinists, persons are rightly held accountable for actions that are "their own"--that is, actions of which they are the sole uncoerced author--and this accords, they maintain, with our actual practice in ethics and law. In seeking to ascertain a person's responsibility, we do not attempt to judge whether her or his action resulted from something called "free will," but simply whether she or he in fact performed the action without external or internal coercion. Admittedly it is difficult in many cases to determine the degree to which a person's behavior in a specific situation is compelled or uncompelled because of what we now know about internal sorts of compulsion; but it is not in principle impossible, soft determinists argue, to work out reasonable guidelines in assessing responsibility. Philosophical soft determinists, such as Antony Flew in his book <u>Crime</u> or <u>Disease?</u>,are concerned to work out criteria for distinguishing relatively coerced from relatively uncoerced actions in the realms of ethics, mental health, and penology. All this is perfectly compatible, they maintain, with a general determinism which subsumes all actions under sufficient causes. Furthermore, the proper function of holding persons responsible for their actions, as for example with punishment, is educative: the object is to reform behavior.[3]

The operant behaviorist B. F. Skinner and some adherents of orthodox psychoanalytic theory are "hard" determinists. The theoretical differences between hard and soft determinists can be clearly delineated, although the practical differences tend to be a matter of degree rather than of kind. Hard determinists accept universal causal explanation and believe that the notions of freedom and responsibility are simply incompatible with it, even though they are often willing to grant a strictly limited, purely functional use to those terms. For a new Augustinian like Skinner, all is truly of "grace": the logic of total determination of human behavior by the interaction of our biological nature and our environment entails that our virtues are no more praiseworthy than our misdeeds are blameworthy. At the same time, he sometimes speaks of freedom in a carefully circumscribed and entirely behavioral way as simply freedom of action, or as a desireable psychological feeling of control over and choice of action regarding one's situation (the "feeling of freedom").[4]

In his much-discussed essay "What Means This Freedom?," the philosopher John Hospers presented the full logic of orthodox psychoanalytic determinism on the matter of freedom and responsibility (although he rejected the determinist label on grounds of conceptual obscurity). He regarded the soft determinist distinction between compelled and uncompelled behavior as untenable on the basis of a psychoanalytic model of behavior emphasizing the dominance of unconscious desires in normal as well as in neurotic behavior. Hospers allowed for a certain purely pragmatic, socially useful notion of responsibility but denied its applicability to the "springs of action."[5]

For the hard determinist, as for the soft determinist, the sole justification for holding persons responsible for their actions is changing their behavior in desireable ways. But whether the application of the concept of responsibility does or does not have such an effect is a matter to be determined on the basis of empirical evidence. On those grounds punishment, Skinner has argued on the basis of his research, is singularly ineffective.[6]

The classical theological Augustinians espoused a version of soft determinism. They believed that the biblical witness required both affirmations-- God's omnipotent control over all events, and human responsibility--though how the two assertions were compatible they confessed was finally a mystery. Their attempts to shed some light on the paradox operated at two levels, the ontological and the empirical. Adam and Eve were created with free will, by which they chose to turn away from the true Center of being and in upon themselves. Their primal sin delivered all their descendants over to unfreedom, to bondage of the will. Nevertheless, since the entire human race exists corporately "in Adam," we are responsible for our condition, guilty before God, and justly objects of divine judgment. With an inscrutable wisdom and love God has eternally elected some to be saved from out of this condition, through no merit of their own but solely and irresistibly by the divine grace. Thus the foundational ontological level. At the empirical level the Augustinians tended to be quite "modern" soft determinists: Although all events are governed by the almighty God and we are furthermore determined by the bondage of original sin, our ordinary evaluations of responsibility in terms of freedom of action are perfectly applicable. We are free at this level insofar as we are able to actualize what we will without coercion or hindrance--free to "do what we will"--and rightly held responsible for such actions. But of course at the deeper ontological level, where God is the sovereign cause of all things and we are bound "in Adam," we are not free to "will what we will."

Clearly such distinctions cannot possibly get an omnipotent and omniscient being off the hook. As Antony Flew pointed out in his rebuttal at the end of the celebrated "Theology and Falsification" symposium, "an omnipotent, omniscient God must be an accessory before (and during) the fact to every human misdeed; as well as being responsible for every non-moral defect in the universe."[7] Even Adam's and Eve's primordial freedom of will was within the divine causal framework, and of course its horribly tragic results were fully within the purview of an eternal knowing which the Augustinians furthermore agreed should not be separated from the eternal willing; yet the fault is all ours and only some will be rescued from everlasting hell. Wrestling with the issue out of both the dramatically transforming experiences of the divine grace and power in their lives and what they believed to be the irresistible logic of the biblical testimony to the divine omnipotence and omniscience, the Augustinian theologians memorably followed out the violently paradoxical consequences in all their splendor and appallingness. To the religious and moral objections which they themselves knew so well and spent considerable effort in answering, they finally counselled bowing in humility before the inscrutable mystery of the infinite God and scolded everyone roundly for creaturely presumption in calling the Creator to account. After all the illuminating and necessary explanations have been given, we must at the deepest level simply accept in reverent awe both that God determines all events, including our own salvation, and that we are also corporately guilty and individually responsible for our actions.

Augustine himself, the fountainhead and perennial inspiration of the tradition, handled all the issues with sovereign thoroughness and a superb mind. The way he develops the logic of omnipotence in a work such as the Enchiridion, forthrightly facing all the hardest texts and issues and reconciling all in an architectonic synthesis, is by sheer aesthetic standards a thing of remarkable balance and grandeur.[8] And the foundation of the edifice is that "nothing...happens unless the Omnipotent wills it to happen. He either allows it to happen or actually causes it to happen."[9] But even the category of allowing things to happen that are against God's will, as in the crucial case of human sin, is covered by the divine willing, since "surely his permission is not unwilling but willing."[10] Yet humanity is a mass of condemnation, and justly so, because of Adam's primal free act of rebellion, and God's election of a minority out of this mass to eternal life is pure unqualified grace.

Luther was inclined to be reticent about the full import of the Augustinian position. Even in his strongest attack on the notion of free will, The Bondage of the Will, he distinguished between the "preached" and the "secret" will of God. He acknowledged that while from a total theological point of view we must affirm the sovereign determination by God of all events, with the irreconcilable paradoxes it poses for Christianity, at the existential level we must simply cling to and proclaim the active will of God for the salvation of sinners and God's all-sufficiency in turning us from sin and justifying us in Christ.

Calvin, by contrast, returned to Augustine's style of complete forthrightness, believing that it was vital precisely at the practical, existential level to set forth the full counsel of God. For Calvin the affirmation of the ultimate determination of all events by the infinite God, whatever the theoretical paradoxes it produced, was a supreme source of assurance and hope to the believer. The chapters on the divine providence in Book I of the

Institutes eloquently embody Calvin's very biblical[12] and pastoral treatment of the subject. His vigorous argument against the notions of fortune and chance in a world governed in its minutest detail by the personal will of the Creator is a particularly powerful affirmation of total cosmic meaningfulness--that profound and sustaining sense of place and direction underlying religious determinism before which the modern alienated mind boggles.

Of all the Augustinian theologians, Jonathan Edwards in his Freedom of the Will was the most thoroughgoing and fully consistent exponent of theological determinism. The eighteenth-century genius was also the most "modern" in his treatment of the subject, brilliantly reworking Calvinist theology in the light of early modern philosophical and scientific knowledge. Edwards was mystically overwhelmed by contemplation of the infinite, eternal, omnipotent, omniscient Being whose creative power and wisdom brings into being out of nothingness and alone sustains the whole universe of myriad creatures visible and invisible. To Edwards it was metaphysically preposterous to think that there was anything whatsoever, whether in the "natural" or in the "moral" order, that did not have a necessary and sufficient cause. "So that it is indeed as repugnant to reason, to suppose an act of the will should come into existence without a cause, as to suppose the human soul, or an angel, or the globe of the earth, or the whole universe, should come into existence without a cause."[13] As for the Arminian notion that the will is self-determined, Edwards attempted to show that the very concept of self-determination is riddled with contradictions.

The alternative to self-determination is other-determination. Edwards' analysis of human behavior might be called "environmental," in Skinner's sense of the total environing field--physical, social, linguistic--to which human behavior is a response. According to Edwards, volitionally the human mind is determined by the strongest among the various "motives" that it perceives. A motive is any sort of fact--or environmental contingency or set of contingencies, if you will--perceived as an object of choice or preference. Volition or "willing" is inseparable from motivation so understood. In his classic study of Edwardean theology, Piety Versus Moralism, Joseph Haroutunian, writing in the heyday of the earlier (and less sophisticated) Watsonian behaviorism, made this striking observation about Edwards' theory of motives:

A modern rendering of this analysis is the study of human behavior in terms of "stimulus and response." A stimulus is Edwards' "motive," and response is volitional behavior. Such a study is based upon the principle that where there is no stimulus, there is no response; where there is no action, there is no reaction; where there is no cause, there is no effect. The nature of a given stimulus is irrelevant to the fact that it acts as a stimulus. An "S-R bond" may be physical or it may be moral, and in both cases it is a "certain connection" between a "motive" and an act of volition. Edwards' metaphysical principle of necessity is the modern methodological principle that all action is reaction.[14]

Like the other Augustinians, Edwards considered the soft-determinist definition of freedom merely as freedom from coercion to be the only coherent and usable one: "power, opportunity or advantage, that any one has, to do as he pleases."[15] I am free insofar as I am able to carry out in action without impediment what I prefer to do. But of course what I prefer to do is determined by the strongest motive that presents itself. It is certainly the case that I may or may not be able in any given circumstances to do as I please, but it is not the case that I am similarly able or not able to "please as I please."

2. Self-determinism

Now libertarians[16]--defenders of free will, whom we might best call "self-determinists" rather than the usual but perhaps misleading term "indeterminists"--regard hard determinism as more consistent with determinist assumptions than soft determinism; but of course they also believe that determinism generally is mistaken at least with regard to some human choices. Self-determinists

48

believe (rightly) against the soft determinists that "uncoerced" is not all we mean by "free" in ethical and legal contexts. At bottom, they argue, when we say that a person "could have done otherwise" we mean that she or he "could genuinely have chosen otherwise given precisely her or his character and the same circumstances." In other words, we include in our ordinary language about human behavior not only freedom of action but also freedom of will; and at least in some instances, say the libertarians, this accurately describes the actual situation. Thus the soft determinist assertion that our ordinary language about freedom is compatible with a general determinism is wrong, as its general determinism is also wrong.
.

Freedom of will refers to the capacity of the human self to choose as a causal agent whose choice is not sufficiently accounted for in terms of the interaction of character and situation. On this view at least some human decisions and actions are intrinsically and not merely contingently not-fully-predictable; the human agent is at least on occasion the creator of the irreducibly novel. The philosopher-theologian John Hick very aptly describes this concept of freedom with reference to the central issue whether a person's formed character is the source of all her or his dispositions and actions: "...whilst a free action arises out of the agent's character it does not arise in a fully determined and predictable way. It is largely but not fully prefigured in the previous stage of the agent. For the character is itself partially formed and sometimes partially re-formed in the very moment of decision."[17]

Significantly, very few self-determinists can be characterized as "hard." The most notable example of hard indeterminism[18] is Jean-Paul Sartre, who in Being and Nothingness argued for the radical view that human beings are free in all their actions and therefore responsible for their entire existence. He based his view on a phenomenological analysis of the intentionality of consciousness. Consciousness, he believed, is an "original spontaneity" which inherently constitutes itself as other than--as the negation of--all objects of consciousness both external and internal (including the ego-self).

Except among his existentialist followers, Sartre's theory of radical freedom has never gained wide currency despite its initially bracing appeal to many students of existentialism. The phenomenological analysis of consciousness, of which Sartre's is one significant example, has produced fundamentally important insights into the nature and function of human awareness, as I noted with regard to Viktor Frankl's work in Chapter One. But Sartre's own translation of the structural intentionality of consciousness into the language of freedom and responsibility is both methodologically dubious and also appears to fly in the face of a wealth of empirical evidence which plainly suggests that there is a great deal of genuine and not merely "inauthentic" bondage in human behavior.

But virtually all other forms of self-determinist analysis are of the "soft" variety. Most libertarians readily concede that genuinely free acts are comparatively rare; that a very large portion of our behavior is in principle sufficiently explicable in terms of the genetic and environmental causes that produce what we call a person's character. Self-determinists also recognize what is obvious: that the capacity for and exercise of freedom seems to be very unevenly (and should I add, with a nod to theology, "unfairly"?) distributed among humans and itself grounded in our individual natures and environments. In one of the best-argued cases for a libertarian view that have come to my attention, my friend and former colleague J. Edward Barrett wrote the following:

> Much of human life is lived--and perhaps all of it can be lived--on subhuman levels of existence, in which the self merely acknowledges the stronger genetically programmed or historically conditioned claim. The freedom of the human self to press claims of its own may remain an undeveloped potential, grow weak from insufficient exercise, or be ineffective due to lack of expertise. Its ability to command authority understandably varies among men and within the history of the individual man. The strength of the

presiding self is biochemically grounded and is also biochemically unstable.[19]

Furthermore, most self-determinists grant that it is difficult to establish criteria for and to identify genuinely free acts in contrast to unfree ones.

One of the most distinguished and persuasive philosophical exponents of free will in this century, the British philosopher C. A. Campbell, spoke of the necessity frankly to recognize "that there is a wide area of human conduct, determinable on clear general principles, within which free will does not effectively operate." He went on to say that "there are an almost immeasureably greater number of situations in a man's life that conform to this [determined] pattern than there are in which an agent [can be said to act freely]...."[20]

Campbell attempted to establish and characterize that "small sector" of genuinely free decisions through phenomenological analysis of moral decision making. His argument rests on the internal distinction he believes we experience between the self as our formed (determined) character and the self as (free) moral decision maker.

> For the very function of moral effort, as it appears to the agent engaged in the act, is to enable the self to act against the line of least resistance, against the line to which his character as so far formed most strongly inclines him. But if the self is thus conscious here of combating his formed character, he surely cannot possibly suppose that the act, although his own act, issues from his formed character?...
>
> What this implies...is that the nature of the self is for itself something more than just its character as so far formed.... The "nature" of the self comprehends, but is not without remainder reducible to, its "character"....[21]

But Campbell's effort, carefully argued and circumscribed though it is, does not, I think, succeed. It does not succeed because it is entirely plausible to interpret the capacity of a particular self to resist its inclinations in favor of its duty as itself a character trait. It is a fact of common observation that there are all shades and degrees of moral sensitivity among human beings. Some persons are preoccupied with and reflective and careful about moral decisions; others are not. We recognize persons who habitually strive to attend to what they believe to be their moral responsibilities and not simply to their inclinations as exhibiting a certain sort of character. Freud and others have shed some light on the sorts of factors in childhood that can tend to produce this sort of character. They also illuminate the neurotically obsessive forms that are the distortions of a serious sense of conscience and moral duty. My awareness of wrestling with my character as thus far formed--with my "natural" inclinations--need not be interpreted as a distinction between self and character, but simply as an internal struggle that "characterizes" some persons much of the time and many persons at least some of the time.

3. The New Augustinianism of B. F. Skinner

I want now specifically to look at some aspects of B. F. Skinner's behaviorist philosophy[22] against the background of my discussion of theological and secular forms of Augustinianism. I focus on Skinner because I believe that his work and its widespread practical influence in behavior modification techniques in education, mental health, and penal programs represent one of the most significant models of human nature and behavior in our time. Operant behaviorism poses a philosophical and theological challenge which must be taken seriously and responded to constructively and integratively.

Thirty years after its publication, Walden Two remains, I think, the best introduction to Skinner himself and to the spirit of his behaviorism.[23] The utopian novel reveals more fully than any of his nonfiction writings do Skinner's humanity and humanism, his wide reading and admirable literacy, his wit and imagination, his loves and aversions.

In personal passion it much surpasses his autobiography.[24] Walden Two also has the important virtue of making appealingly clear the fully human face that "behavior mod" has always had for Skinner and his followers, over against the sinister, machinal caricature so widely held. The book lets us view the principles and practice of operant behaviorism ideally at work among normal human beings concretely interacting in a total social and cultural setting that is the overall product of behavioral design. In the course of the story Skinner touches on a remarkable number of issues large and small (including ample doses of philosophy, religion, and politics), gives specific examples of behavior-changing techniques, and exhibits an appreciation of the subtleties and nuances in actual human behavior that is less apparent in his other books. In one way (but only one!) he reminds me of Walter Kaufmann's characterization of some of the existentialist writers: he seems to state his position more clearly and compellingly in fiction than in technical discussion.[25]

To elaborate somewhat digressively on the point: I have become convinced that the only way properly and fully to appreciate Skinner is in terms of complementary or alternative languages: that is, two different ways of describing the same phenomena. In his strictly scientific works such as Science and Human Behavior and Contingencies of Reinforcement[26] he develops his theories in a generalized scientific language that achieves accuracy at the expense of the reader's ability to relate it all to her or his concrete experience as a complex subject interacting with other subjects. By contrast, in Walden Two, in published interviews, and in television appearances Skinner warmly and imaginatively fleshes out the theories in the existential language of personal, social, and cultural situations--a language that enables the reader or viewer much more readily to grasp and above all sympathetically to appreciate operant behaviorism. One can certainly understand why Skinner, who perceives himself as a rigorously empirical scientist, uses two such different languages to present his views; but he has invited a great deal of hostility and misunderstanding by not relating the two much more closely and explicitly.

The gap is by no means absolute, especially in a work such as his semi-popular book <u>Beyond</u> <u>Freedom</u> <u>and</u> <u>Dignity</u>. Yet even there, the dominant language is decidedly abstractive and generalized. Precisely because Skinner is describing and interpreting that most complex and controversial of all phenomena, human nature and behavior, the translation from scientific to existential language is essential to a full understanding of and a fair hearing for operant behaviorism.

Novelists standardly warn us not to identify them with any of their characters or with particular viewpoints they express. As it happens, however, we have Skinner's own word for it, in an article in the <u>American</u> <u>Psychologist</u> in 1956, that his protagonist Frazier is to a large degree a spokesman for himself, allowing him freewheelingly and imaginatively to explore all sorts of ideas unconstrained by the limitations of strictly scientific exposition. Even without such an explicit confirmation by the author, the reader is very inclined to infer such an identification from the clearly didactic--indeed, evangelical--tone of the book (which is also the source of its artistic flaws). There is no reason to believe that Frazier's remarks about all sorts of matters do not reflect something of Skinner's own thinking.

In <u>Walden</u> <u>Two</u> Skinner indulges in a bit of fun directed, I think, at both himself and his critics. Frazier confesses that, as the designer of the Walden Two community, he "likes to play God" and jokingly but not altogether facetiously compares himself both to the Creator-Father and to Christ the Son. At one point his posture even mimics Jesus on the cross. Frazier remarks that "'In many ways the creation of Walden Two was closer to the spirit of Christian cosmogony than the evolution of the world according to modern science'"[27]--that is, Walden Two was brought into being by Frazier's purposeful design; it did not evolve hit-and-miss. The "science of behavior"--Skinner's operant behaviorism--enables Frazier to design the community so that he knows what the consequences of each aspect of its design will be, just as in traditional theology it is according to God's eternal plan and purpose that the universe as a whole and in all its parts unfolds. Frazier explicitly goes on to relate this creation analogy to what he calls "the old question of predestination and free will." As he describes it to Burris (who is perhaps Burrhus Frederic Skinner's alter ego):

"All that happens is contained in an original plan, yet at every stage the individual seems to be making choices and determining the outcome. The same is true of Walden Two. Our members are practically always doing what they want to do--what they 'choose' to do--but we see to it that they will want to do precisely the things which are best for themselves and the community. Their behavior is determined, yet they're free."[28]

Frazier here links Walden Two's "behavioral engineering" and classical theological determinism. At the beginning of this essay I introduced Skinner's explicit and robust determinism. While granting that determinism is unproveable, he claims that it is both axiomatic for and continually vindicated by scientific inquiry. Frazier puts it unmistakeably: "'I deny that freedom exists at all . . . . Perhaps we can never _prove_ that man isn't free; it's an assumption. But the increasing success of a science of behavior makes it more and more plausible.'"[29]

There is of course no contradiction in Frazier's assertion and then denial of freedom in the two passages just cited. In the first he uses "free" approvingly to refer to freedom of action: being able to do what one wants to do. In the second he rejects the term "freedom" insofar as it refers to free will: the idea of a causal agent, a personal author of actions, whose agency is necessarily but not sufficiently accounted for by its antecedent conditions. This distinction is an example of the practical similarity that can exist between hard and soft determinism. Skinner also talks at times of the desireability of persons' "feeling free": feeling that they are in some basic sense in control of their life, that their decisions and actions make a difference.

According to Skinner's behaviorism, all human behavior results from the interaction between genetic endowment and environmental contingencies. He grants that human actions are highly complex and that frequently we cannot predict them accurately because of the many factors involved. But he believes that all actions are predictable in principle, and furthermore is convinced by the actual successes of behavior modification experiments that we can empirically learn enough of the relevant factors to bring about and predict desired behavior.

As Frazier's remarks and other references in his writings indicate, Skinner is well aware at least in broad outlne of the tradition of theological determinism in Christianity. It has long seemed to me that theologians, perhaps more than any other humanistically-oriented inquirers, should be able from out of their own biblical and theological tradition to appreciate and integrate the picture of our utter creatureliness and total interdependence that Skinner depicts in his admittedly offputting, narrowly physicalist conceptual scheme and terminology. Those who are scandalized by Skinner's behavioral determinism should again recall that central elements in the biblical and theological portrayals of the Creator and the Creator's relationship to his/her creatures have provided the basis for the impressive Augustinian tradition of theological determinism.

There are serious criticisms to be made of Skinner's theories that should be noted here. They include (among others) unexamined assumptions and unwarranted inferences, his apparent insensitivity to the inherent limitations of any theoretical model, and his methodological tunnel vision. There is also an explanatory superficiality about his work which is closely related to these other defects. While there would seem ostensibly to be a theoretical advantage in Skinner's application of the principle of parismony to human behavior--for example, attempting to avoid what he considers "unnecessary" explanatory entities such as mind and mental events--the end result is suspiciously thin as an overall account of what these highly complex beings called persons are and why they do what they do. For all their speculative tendencies, the explanations of behavior advanced by the great depth psychologists like Freud and Jung were perhaps in an important sense more scientific at least in probing behind appearances and attempting a detailed etiology of the human phenomenon.

For all that, Skinner's analysis of behavior in, say Science and Human Behavior, Contingencies of Reinforcement, and Beyond Freedom and Dignity is considerably more subtle than his detractors give it credit for being. Typical critiques of Skinner's theories, such as Arthur Koestler's in The Ghost in the Machine [30] and The Call Girls, [31] are little more than caricatures. They persist in simply identifying Skinner's operant behaviorism with the less sophisticated pioneering behaviorism of Pavlov and Watson. It does not seem to matter to Koestler and other caricaturists that Skinner's theory of behavior is considerably more complex than the old stimulus-response views, and that he explicitly points out his differences from Pavlov and Watson.

As a matter of fact, Skinner's theory is at least in principle a highly complex picture of human nature and behavior. To say that our actions are the product of genetic and environmental interaction is to imply a very great deal--more than Skinner's own tendency to generalization and simplification usually suggests. Skinner himself recognizes that there is still an enormous amount we do not know about the genetic code and its specific workings, while our involvement with our physical and social environmental context contains more factors than we can possibly identify. At the same time, behavior modificationists definitely believe that out of the total complex of factors determining behavior we can know and select enough relevant environmental reinforcers to enable us consciously and systematically to alter our behavior in terms of specific individual and cultural goals. But along with this confidence, in the case of both Skinner and many other operant behaviorists, usually goes an appropriate sense of fallibility and a very open and experimental attitude toward behavioral design.

It should be obvious to each of us upon reflection that our decisions and actions are responses to the world around us. These responses can be highly creative or simply reactive--and Skinner fully acknowledges that our relationship to our environment is not simply passive but also quite active. The issue is the nature of the creative responses, the ones at least some of which the libertarian wants to call "free." Do they manifest a causal agent for which this complex genetic-environmental situation is a sufficient reason, or does the causal agent produce something which is not fully reducible to this total context? Skinner of course maintains the former. He does not see how there can be events for which there are not in principle sufficient reasons. And of course, as David Hume's discussion of free will in An Inquiry Concerning Human Understanding made clear a long time ago, so long as we do not have complete knowledge of all the factors involved in human behavior, the determinist will always regard the burden of proof as resting with the self-determinist.[32] The former sees the concept of free will as simply a stop-gap for our ignorance, not a defensible notion.

In depth and explanatory power, the psychoanalytic tradition remains a far more illuminating interpretation of human bondage, one that (in good "Augustinian" fashion) graphically accounts for the deep-rooted and demonic aspects of that bondage over against Skinner's irrepressible optimism. Nevertheless, his single-minded scientific labors, in spotlighting what is surely the enormously important role of environmental reinforcers in human behavior, are of great practical usefulness in understanding and helping persons. Skinner's work also forms yet another essential piece in that whole puzzle of human nature and behavior which philosophers and theologians are obliged to integrate into a realistic picture of human life and the cosmos.

4. Freedom and Responsibility: A Proposal

Until comparatively recently my own analysis of freedom and responsibility led me to a cautious defense of a kind of "minimal self-determinism." It seemed to me that the data of experience and the

58

problematic status of the deterministic hypothesis demanded a general openness to the possibility of insufficiently determined human choices. At the same time, however, I concluded that genuinely free choices were probably very infrequent and--most important of all--completely elusive to identification. As a corollary of the elusiveness and "hiddenness" of free choices I began to develop a purely pragmatic justification of the vital notion of responsibility.[33]

Continued pondering of the issues, however, has caused me to revise my approach to the problem of freedom. Whether "soft" or "hard," the deterministic picture of human behavior now appears to me to be decisively more clear-eyed about our condition than the libertarian affirmations of human freedom. I hasten to add that I do not equate "clear-eyed" with "fully adequate." On philosophical grounds, I do not see how determinism can be anything more than a heuristic, metaphysical, or theological assumption. Heuristically it has certainly been one of the most massively fruitful of all presuppositional principles in human thought generally and in the development of scientific knowledge in particular. But on scientific grounds themselves, universal causal determinism has been seriously challenged in the twentieth century, as for example by the principle of indeterminacy in physics and by hierarchic-evolutionary models of organic development and function in biology.[34]

But the force of deterministic analyses of behavior does not depend on their deterministic assumptions but on their clear recognition of the empirical reality of an indefinitely large measure of behavioral determination by the interaction of our biological natures and our social-physical environments. Recent scientific demurrers on determinism still grant an extremely high degree of causal explanation and predictability in events. Indeterminacy at the subatomic level is negligible in its effects on the explanation and prediction of macroscopic behavior, while spontaneity in the growth and function of living organisms appears to be a very limited randomness within the interaction between genetic blueprint and environmental context. What the enthusiasts for novelty and spontaneity in these elements of the world-process always seem to me to neglect is the strictly limited scope and activity of these seemingly acausal factors. Most importantly, the fullblown concept of freedom at the human level, while often grounded in the "inner-ness" or internal spontaneity that is believed to characterize organic processes and events,[35] is the idea of something significantly different from a general indeterminacy. It is the concept of a fully conscious, intelligent, deliberative, purposive agent. The self-determinist does not equate human freedom with spontaneous activity, with randomness or chance. The idea of free will is much more clearly defined and restricted in scope to rational and intentional choices--and, of course, we can always observe and inquire into the many factors largely determining the capacity for and exercise of such choices.

a. Potentialities versus Free Will

The sorts of considerations described above have caused me to revise my approach to the problem of freedom. I have come to regard the libertarian attempt to defend and identify free will as an unfruitful effort issuing in negligible and always-problematic results. I believe that the soft-determinst restriction of the terms "free" and "freedom" to freedom of action is normatively useful if not descriptively complete. I am inclined to recommend that we confine our talk about freedom to its empirical applications, in which relative absence of coercion or compulsion is the criterion. Thus persons released from jail, citizens of a democracy, persons who are economically secure, decisions made reflectively with external pressure at a minimum, intellectual inquiry unfettered by ideological restrictions, and mentally healthy persons are different but readily recognizeable applications of the term "free" in various senses of "relatively uncoerced."

At the level of the "springs of action," I now prefer to talk not about free will but rather about empirical possibilities or potentialities. The human personality is a highly complex reality constantly responding to a social environment that

60

is also complex and always changing. While our basic individual behavior patterns can be illuminated and predicted through psychological investigation, in most particular situations the full range of our repertoire of possible responses is at least partly hidden both from ourselves and from others. For certain individual personalities and in certain sorts of contexts the range of such potentialities is doubtless severely limited; for other personalities and in other sorts of situations it may be quite broad. My point is simply that neither the agent nor the observer/interactor knows, except in some cases in terms of general parameters of behavior, the complete repertoire at any given time. Even if all behavior is the product of the interaction of character and environment, what constitutes a person's character is never completely transparent and the environmental factors to which character responds are always fluid and novel. For the person who is actually in the concrete situation of decision-making and for those who are interacting with or observing that person, both present and future are empirically "open" in their texture of possibilites.

But of course our behavioral possibilities are to an indeterminably large degree shaped by our nature and nurture, and are always circumscribed by that framework. Our very partial knowledge of our repertoires of possibilities is a function of the great complexity and changingness of the configuration personality-responding-to-environment; it is not an argument for acausality or underdetermination of human actions. The moral challenge that seems to me to be posed by the recognition of both the bondage and the potentialities in human behavior is to achieve a delicate balance in our relationships with and understanding of persons. It is to respond compassionately to the unknowably large biological-environmental "givenness" in my own and others' character and actions, while at the same time nurturing and challenging the often unknown and suprising possibilities that are ours within those givens. This is admittedly a difficult balance to strike because of our deep-rooted assumptions about free will, our very imperfect knowledge, and the conscious and unconscious needs we bring to our

61

involvement with other persons. Nonetheless, it is just such a balanced response to persons that the data of human behavior demand of those who are able to respond--and of course none of us knows whether and to what degree we can so respond until we actually make a serious and repeated effort.

Contemporary knowledge of human nature and action gives new force to the commandment to love my neighbor as myself. It is typically the case that I rationalize my own behavior--in part, that I excuse it with causal or determining explanations: "I've had a bad day," or "It's just the way I am." At the same time, I tend not to excuse other persons in this way but to hold them fully responsible for their actions. In other words, generally speaking I am a determinist with regard to myself and a self-determinist with regard to others. To love others as myself means, in part, that I must be compassionate enough to recognize in their actions the determining factors that I recognize--albeit often self-servingly--in my own life.

The balanced response of love also demands, however, that I recognize, challenge, and nurture, both in others and in myself, in a quite unmoralistic way, those hidden potentialities that are a never-fully-predictable source of creative response-ability. The elusiveness of our possibilities within a heavily determined character structure should make us charitable in our judgments about other persons and ourselves; but that same elusiveness renders us responsive to challenge and nurture in unforeseen ways.

b. A Pragmatic Justification of Responsibility

I continue to believe that the idea of responsibility is both defensible and necessary on purely pragmatic grounds, quite apart from the problematic notion of free will. Clearly, holding persons responsible for their actions, demanding that they assume responsibility for their behavior, can be humanly beneficial in the realms of ethics, mental health, and law. I emphasize the "can be," because it also seems clear that the practice of holding persons responsible is widely abused, as when it manifests self-righteousness, vengefulness, ignorance, and insensitivity. Appropriate forms of making persons accountable for certain actions are those which not only (1) determine that they are in fact the agent of the actions but also (2) genuinely hope by calling them to account to elicit an affirmative response that betokens desireable behavior change at least regarding that situation. This may also require (3) the development of the most behaviorally effective means of ascribing responsibility to persons in various contexts of action.

On this whole matter I am of course in agreement with the deterministic analyses of responsibility that I presented earlier in this essay. However, soft determinists seem more conoerned simply to justify our ordinary practice of holding persons responsible and less interested in what should be the most important upshot of their pragmatic interpretation of accountability in terms of reform or education: the problem of when and how to hold persons responsible in such a way that it actually reforms and educates. Hard determinists like Skinner appear to me to be at least formally correct in urging us to clarify empirically and experimentally, insofar as possible, what sorts of applications of responsibility to other persons genuinely contribute to desireable behavior change and what sorts are counterproductive. Granted the pragmatic justification of holding most persons answerable for their actions in various situations, an important task for psychologists, mental health professionals, and penologists is to help us by shedding some light on just what sorts of ascriptions of responsibility are truly pragmatic-- that is, really "work" humanely in human life.

But of course such a task is a difficult one and perhaps admissible of only very approximate guidelines and methods because of the partly opaque complexity of the person and the partly novel situations to which she or he is always responding. The problem of responsibility is bound up with the hiddenness of our potentialities within the formidable matrix of genetic-environmental shaping. Is calling agent A_1 to account in situation S_1 useful or useless? To what extent is A_1 capable of acknowledging her or his responsibility in the situation? To what extent will being held responsible for S_1 affect A_1's behavior? These are questions the answers to which we usually do not have. We probably do well as a rule of thumb to hold persons responsible for their actions in many situations, but we often simply do not know its effects. Nevertheless, I think it is possible, on the basis of the psychological knowledge we have of types and patterns of behavior, to acquire some practical wisdom regarding when and how to ascribe responsibility to persons.

Of special interest to me is the central importance of holding myself responsible for my actions. A classical and widely-agreed-upon character ideal in both ethics and psychology is the "responsible self," the person who habitually and healthily assumes responsibility for her or his behavior. We properly associate such an attitude with maturity, autonomy, and integrity, and seek to develop it in our children. Obviously there are neurotic forms of holding oneself responsible, as in the case of a person's obsessive guilt over all sorts of things for which she or he is not in fact accountable; but I am looking now at its healthy forms. What particularly absorbs me is the phenomenon that I call the "paradox of responsibility": the active assumption of responsibility for their life and actions by persons who are fully and knowledgeably aware of the formidable role of genetic and environmental factors in shaping them into the sorts of persons they are.

I am acutely aware of the degree to which my parents' behavior patterns have been transmitted to me; I struggle frustratingly with those that I do not like in myself, only to see them emerge again and again, compulsively, against my will, in my behavior in very predictable ways. Yet I firmly believe that it is the mark of maturity and integrity not to excuse myself for those behaviors but to own them as my own and to struggle with them. It is not a matter of being "hard on myself" about characteristics I seemingly cannot do much about. I accept that I have been profoundly shaped in these ways; it is simply that I do not interpret the shaping as something alien, something "from outside" myself that excuses me. That is an example of the paradox of responsibility. This phenomenon especially illuminates the wholly practical nature and justification of holding persons responsible. It is highly beneficial to my growth as a mature human being to accept responsibility in a healthy way not only for particular actions but also for my life as a whole, even though what I am is at least very largely the product of nature and nurture and the issue of free will is at least very problematic.

I must say at least a brief word about what effect considerations of legal justice have on the justification for holding persons responsible that I have presented. I refer specifically to the problem of actions that harm other persons, whether through deprivation of what is rightfully theirs or through mental or physical injury. In my view, justice demands the alleviation of the victim's plight or the restitution of her or his loss, insofar as possible. The person who caused the harm, the author of the actions, is clearly the one who should be required to alleviate or make some form of restitution if she or he is mentally and physically competent to do so. This obligation holds entirely independently of the question whether it will change the offender's behavior, precisely because there is someone besides the offender involved. Our moral and legal duties to other human beings bind us regardless of whether they do us any good or not, and this is specifically highlighted in the case of caring for or compensating victims of harm.

It may be noticed that I have said nothing about justice demanding incarceration in the case of legally defined harm, but only restitution and alleviation. There is one and only one justification for imprisonment: to protect society from repeated committers of violent crimes (armed robbery, rape, assault, murder). On the basis of the analysis of the problem of human freedom that I have presented, I find the notion of incarceration as punishment entirely unjustified, unless it can be shown that punishment changes behavior for the better. The evidence that imprisonment, given the actual conditions of prisons, does not do that--in fact, in many cases has the opposite effect--is overwhelming. Even for persons who have repeatedly done bodily harm to others, there is no justification for the conditions of incarceration to be as grim as possible, but only for society to be protected. For first offenders and persons who commit non-violent crimes (unarmed robbery, fraud, embezzlement, forgery, and the like), incarceration is <u>unjust</u> as well as unproductive in altering their behavior. Justice, as I see it, is served only by requiring the offenders to make restitution for or help alleviate what they have done to their victims; this applies to the violent offender who must be incarcerated for public safety as well as to the non-violent offender. The notion that imprisonment has anything intrinsically to do with justice is a historical and cultural fixation that must be described as not only erroneous but also barbarous. Admittedly, making restitution to the victim is a very imperfect thing at best; some harms, especially assaults on the person with the mental anguish and physical impairment that they can produce, simply cannot be compensated for. But there are many ways in which at least a substantial token of recompense can be enacted by the offender, and only a poverty of imagination stands in the way of devising them.

As a matter of fact, requiring offenders to make some sort of restitution may, if it is rightly done, be an effective means of changing their behavior for the better. The thief who is required to do a substantial amount of supervised but useful and adequately compensated labor directed toward repaying at least a portion of what he or she has stolen may cease to be a thief. The chances seem to me far better that restitution and alleviation will reform and educate than that imprisonment will. If such is the case, then that is an added benefit.

But as I have said, the demand for restitution or alleviation is inherent in the reality of the social consequences of our actions, quite apart from whether the demand improves the offender or not. Holding persons responsible for their actions at this level is simply the minimal and quite incomplete first step in the full notion of accountability: determining that <u>A</u> is in fact the one who did the deed in question. Whether or not <u>A</u> could "help" doing what she or he did or not, whether <u>A</u> had the possibility of doing otherwise, is

not the point at issue on the plane of justice.
Since A harmed someone else, A is properly the
person who is to be required to make restitution if
she or he is able. Ideally, of course, both the
demands of justice and the full notion of
accountability should come into play: A is the one
who should make recompense, and the method of
compensation should be designed to minimize the
possibility that A will offend in that way again.

5. Human Bondage and Moral Evil

A rightly serious and urgent question that
always arises in connection with the problem of
freedom and responsibility is, What about moral
evil, especially in its worst forms? Any view that
dispenses with the notion of free will and argues
for a purely pragmatic notion of responsibility
would appear to be unable to take a Hitler, let us
say, with the moral seriousness that we
spontaneously manifest in our concrete existence.
If we must talk only about Hitler's bondage to the
forces that produced him and about his particular
repertoire of potentialities, do we not excuse his
appallingly heinous crimes? If holding persons
responsible is simply a matter of ascertaining who
did the deed and possibly changing her or his
behavior, do we not again let the Austrian madman
off the hook? Do not all deterministic and quasi-
deterministic accounts of moral behavior offend our
natural sense of justice?

The first thing to be said in reply is that
moral evil does not become less evil because we
cannot identify it as the product of something
called "free will." It is still just as real, it
must still be resisted. Whatever produced Hitler's
sadistic vision of reality and the decisions that
flowed from it, Nazism was a monstrous threat to
human life and dignity and freedom (in its properly
empirical senses) and had to be stopped. The second
observation is this: Hitler was clearly
"responsible" for his crimes in the basic factual
sense that he was indeed their author; the evidence
for that is overwhelming. But of course that is a
necessary but far from sufficient sense of "being
responsible." The more crucial question is, What
were Hitler's actual possibilities of doing other

67

than he did within the character boundaries that his nature and nurture had produced? To what extent was he actually amenable to moral suasion and accountability? We simply do not know. We quite naturally condemn him as a moral monster, as one of history's arch-criminals; but what do these judgments have to do with settling the question as to the causes of his behavior?

Indeed, for many years we have been familiar with various psychiatric evaluations of Hitler, virtually all of which see his behavior as pathological and some of which declare it psychotic. Terms like "megalomania" and "paranoia" are standard in treatments of Hitler; the common term "madman" came naturally to me in an earlier paragraph, as I am sure it does to a great many people. When we go on to reflect on other particularly terrible cases of moral evil, the same sorts of clinical and popular judgements are made: Caligula, Jack the Ripper, Charles Manson, Son of Sam. As a matter of fact, it is precisely such appalling forms of moral evil that we are most inclined to attribute to psychological pathologies; no "normal" person, we usually say, could do such things. But defenders of free will typically associate it with normal rational-moral acts, not with abnormal behavior. If we wish to affirm free will, it does not seem to me that we can have it both ways: free will cannot simultaneously be associated with normality and mental health and ascribed to a Hitler.

What "secular Augustinian" analyses of freedom and responsibility such as mine can do with regard to the question of moral evil is to help us clarify an important distinction that must be made. That is the distinction between concrete moral judgments and actions on the one hand, and the question of freedom and responsibility on the other. The former are urgent and proper activities in the existential sphere; the latter, as the whole drift of my essay has tried to show, is the difficult theoretical question of the causes of human behavior. The two modes of discourse intersect at the point of inference from one to the other. We tend to infer from moral judgments about persons and actions common conclusions about free will and accountability which I have tried to show are intrinsically dubious, and are furthermore by no means entailed simply on the basis of our moral judgments. On the other hand, the sorts of considerations I have tried to indicate concerning the problem of freedom and responsibility are of important practical benefit to the concrete business of making moral judgments and taking moral action. By illuminating the depth of our bondage to the forces that shape us and suggesting useful ways in which to understand freedom and accountability, analyses such as the one in this essay can render the language of our moral discourse more informed and sensitive regarding the realities of the human predicament.

FOOTNOTES

[1]N.Y.: Bantam Books.

[2]London: Macmillan, 1973.

[3]Soft determinism is often called the Hume-Mill theory, after its two classical proponents. The paradigmatic twentieth-century statement of soft determinism is Moritz Schlick's "When Is a Man Responsible?," from his Problems of Ethics, trans. by David Rynin, N.Y.: Dover, 1939.

[4]See, e.g., Skinner, op.cit., chs. 5 and 6.

[5]In Sidney Hook, ed., Determinism and Freedom in the Age of Modern Science, N.Y.: Collier, 1958, pp. 126-142.

[6]See, e.g., his discussion of punishment in Science and Human Behavior, N.Y.: The Free Press, 1953, pp. 182-193. The noted trial lawyer Clarence Darrow was a striking example of the consistent application of hard determinism to questions of legal responsibility and punishment, as in his famous summation to the jury in the Leopold-Loeb case. See "The Crime of Compulsion," in Arthur Weinburg, ed., Attorney for the Damned, N.Y.: Simon and Schuster, 1957.

[7]In Flew and Alasdair MacIntyre, eds., New Essays in Philosophical Theology, N.Y.: Macmillan, 1955, p. 107. An interestingly related essay by

Flew in the same volume is "Divine Omnipotence and Human Freedom," pp. 144-169.

[8] In Augustine: Confessions and Enchiridion, newly translated and edited by Albert C. Outler, vol. VII of the Library of Christian Classics, Philadelphia: The Westminister Press, n.d.. See esp. Chs. XXIV-XXIX.

[9] P. 395.

[10] P. 399.

[11] In Luther and Erasmus: Free Will and Salvation, De Servo Arbitrio translated and edited by Philip S. Watson in collaboration with B. Drewery, vol. XVII of the Library of Christian Classics, Philadelphia: The Westminster Press, 1969, pp. 101-334.

[12] In Calvin: Institutes of the Christian Religion, edited by John T. McNeill, translated and indexed by Ford Lewis Battles, vol. XX of the Library of Christian Classics, Philadelphia: The Westminster Press, 1960, Book I, Chs. XVII and XVII.

[13] Freedom of the Will, ed., with an introduction, by Arnold S. Kaufman and William K. Frankena, N.Y.: Bobbs-Merrill, 1969, p. 54.

[14] N.Y.: Harper & Row, 1932, p. 225.

[15] Freedom of the Will, pp. 31-32.

[16] Not to be confused with the political theory called libertarianism, which I discuss in Chapter Three. Virtually all political libertarians are also free-will libertarians; but the converse is by no means the case.

[17] In Evil and the God of Love, London: Collins, 1968, p. 312.

[18] Trans. by Hazel E. Barnes, N.Y.: Philosophical Library, 1956.

71

[19] How Are You Programmed?, Richmond: John Knox Press, 1971, p. 26. I disagree with Profesor Barrett's use of the term "subhuman" to describe all behavior that he would regard as unfree.

[20] "Is 'Free Will' a Pseudo-Problem?", in Paul Edwards and Arthur Pap, eds., A Modern Introduction to Philosophy, 3rd ed., N.Y.: The Free Press, 1973, p. 79.

[21] "Has the Self 'Free Will'?", reprinted from On Selfhood and Godhood, N.Y.: Macmillan, 1957, ch. 9: in Raziel Abelson, Ethics and Metaethics, N.Y.: St. Martin's Press, 1963, p. 541.

[22] Skinner explicitly describes his operant behaviorism as a philosophy, in About Behaviorism, N.Y.: Alfred A. Knopf, 1974, p. 3.

[23] N.Y.: Macmillan, 1948.

[24] The first volume has been published as Particulars of My Life, N.Y.: Alfred A. Knopf, 1976.

[25] See Kaufmann's Existentialism from Dostoevsky to Sartre, N.Y.: World, 1956, p. 49.

[26] N.Y.: Appleton-Century-Crofts, 1969.

[27] P. 299.

[28] Walden Two, p. 296-297.

[29] P. 257.

[30] London: Pan Books, 1967. Once he leaves his anti-behaviorist diatribe behind and develops his own creative synthesis of recent biological theory and research, Koestler provides us in The Ghost in the Machine with an exciting alternative model for understanding human behavior.

[31] N.Y.: Dell, 1974. The Call Girls expresses Koestler's deep concerns about human engineering and reductionism in novelistic form--unfortunately, in a very heavy-handed and unrealistic manner.

[32]Ed., with an introduction, by Charles W. Hendel, N.Y.: Bobbs-Merrill, 1955, Section VIII.

[33]This analysis characterized my approach in "The Elusiveness of Freedom and Some Implications," Journal of Social Philosophy, vol. x, no. 1, Jan. 1974, pp. 13-16; and in "Listening to B. F. Skinner," The Christian Century, vol. XCIV, no. 39, Nov. 30, 1977, pp. 1112-1116.

[34]On indeterminacy, see Werner Heisenberg, Physics and Philosophy, N.Y.: Harper & Brothers, 1958. On holistic biological theory, see Michael Polanyi, Knowing and Being, ed. by Marjorie Grene, Chicago: Univ. of Chicago Press, 1969, pp. 211-239.

[35]Pierre Teilhard de Chardin's interpretation of evolution placed great stress on the development of mind and freedom out of the interiority or "within" of not only organic entities but also atoms and inorganic structures. See The Phenomenon of Man, trans. by Bernard Wall and with an Introduction by Julian Huxley, N.Y.: Harper & Brothers, 1959, esp. Ch. II.

III.

POLITICS FOR NOT-SO-RATIONAL ANIMALS

Over the past decade or so I have followed with interest the resurgence of libertarian thought and activity in the United States. My reading began with Ayn Rand, spread to her schismatic disciple Nathaniel Branden and her distinguished philosophical convert John Hospers, and then broadened out to include the large panoply of libertarian views represented by Reason magazine. The recently-organized Libertarian Party has held national conventions and nominated presidential and vice-presidential candidates in 1972 and 1976, and perhaps constitutes the most serious third-party challenge at the present time. At this writing the ever-fascinating Eugene McCarthy is said to be on very friendly terms with the Libertarian Party. My characterization of libertarianism in this essay is based largely on the libertarian synthesis presented in Murray Rothbard's book For a New Liberty,[1] which a highly informed and active libertarian acquaintance compared upon its publication several years ago with Marx's Communist Manifesto for persuasiveness and (he hoped) historical significance.

Rothbard nicely sums up the "central core of the libertarian creed," on which he believes the whole spectrum of libertarians agrees, as follows: "the absolute right to private property of every man: first, in his own body, and second, in the previously unused natural resources which he first transforms by his labor. These two axioms, the right of self-ownership and the right to 'homestead,' establish the complete set of principles of the libertarian system."[2] Libertarians derive from this "creed" such doctrines as laissez-faire capitalism, a free market of all or almost all goods and services, absolute non-aggression by any person or group against any other, radical criticism of government, and either severe reduction (classical libertarian) or outright aboliton (anarchist libertarian) of its powers.

74

I must confess to being stirred by libertarian literature, particularly of the sort Rothbard writes. No group sounds the theme of individual human freedom the way the libertarians do. Libertarian criticisms of past and existing governments for their arrogance and power-seeking, their everlasting meddling in people's lives and ruthless willingness to sacrifice them to "public interest," their appalling warmaking--all these strike a responsive chord in anyone of reasonable sensibilities who has studied even our own politically advantaged country's history and participated in its life over the past twenty years. Libertarians stand squarely with the most ardent civil-liberties liberals in defending Bill of Rights guarantees and in advocating a maximum of personal liberty[3] on such issues as women's rights, abortion, divorce, conscientious objection, censorship, victimless crimes, treatment of mental patients, and sexual relations between consenting adults. At least Rothbard-style libertarians are just as critical of big business with its mega-corporations and its fawning partnership with the federal government as are many liberals. Liberals who have tended, knee-jerk fashion, to favor governmental solutions to social problems would also do well to learn from libertarian criticisms of such schemes and some of their alternative "private sector" proposals. Finally, there is an admirable consistency about libertarianism which the liberal, with his or her somewhat muddled-moral-pragmatic approach, cannot at times but envy.

What, then, I ask myself, is it that nags at me as I read, say, For a New Liberty? I have no particularly devotional attachment to liberalism; I would gladly be converted to libertarianism if there were compelling reasons. Why, then, even while fascinatedly reading Rothbard, do I end up backing away and continuing to find at least a kind of liberalism more adequate? I do so because there is a flaw at the very foundation of the libertarians' edifice: They have a superficial doctrine of human existence and behavior. In biological and psychological terms, the libertarians seem only very mildly aware that human beings qua human beings are saddled with a heavy genetic-evolutionary, psychic, and environmental burden. In the language of

75

philosophy, they neglect the fact that human life is heavily weighted on the side of "facticity" or destiny.

The libertarian Achilles' heel is the definition of human beings as free and rational animals. The chief spokespersons for libertarianism are avowed rationalists of a more or less Aristotelian sort: Human beings are uniquely the animals who can and must survive by the voluntary exercise of their individual conceptual abilities rather than by instinct. Since we cannot survive in a fully "programmed" manner like other animals, we must each exercise our rational abilities by choice, volitionally. Every normal human being, according to libertarian theoreticians, possesses this basic freedom of rational choice, whatever her or his endowments and circumstances. The assumptions of the essential rationality and the sovereign freedom of the individual form the intellectual foundation of the libertarian creed and the constant theme of libertarian writings.

One basic corollary of libertarian rationalism is adherence to traditional Lockean natural law and natural rights theory. It is the nature of human beings to be the animal whose life and survival depend upon the individual exercise of choice and reasoning. From this flow the individual's absoulte right to her or his own person and to the property (proprius = "one's own") she or he acquires by her or his own labor or by free exchange. One important implication of libertarian rationalism is the assumption that if human individuals are left alone (laissez-faire) with a minimum of interference in their lives and property, a "rational harmony of interests"--to use the eighteenth-century phrase-- will prevail.

To be sure, human beings are uniquely rational in the sense of possessing remarkable cognitive capacities which make possible language, thought, and culture. But the whole point which the libertarian rationalists miss is that from our beginnings until the present day we have overwhelmingly directed this cognitive ability to irrational and supra-rational ends: unconscious desires and conflicts, imaginings and fantasies,

faiths, social myths and ideologies. We seem to
have managed to survive--so far--with a rather
minimal use of that individual, critical, reality-
facing capacity of reason which the libertarians
extol. As Freud wrote, "The voice of intellect is a
soft one." Indeed it is.

I do not want to be misunderstood on this point.
I also agree with the rest of Freud"s statement:
". . . but it does not rest till it has gained a
hearing."[4] Burdened though our cognitive capacities
are by other factors, I believe that the development
of independent, critical reason is one of the most
important achievements of the human species and the
human individual. Every person is obligated to give
that "soft voice" a hearing to the best of her or
his capacities, and the peson who has really done so
is ever after nagged by a creative and fruitful
unrest. Human beings are capable of much more
reasoning than they are usually given credit for or
stimulated to exercise, and every appeal which does
not direct itself to that noble potentiality but
panders instead to human irrationalities is
insulting and exploitative. It nevertheless remains
the case that in fact this soft voice of reason
operates under severe limitations and in the context
of powerful non-rational forces which simply must be
taken into account in a full characterization of
human behavior.

The problem of freedom is intimately connected.
Human beings are in some sense uniquely
characterized by a wide range of potentialities but
we are by no means possessed of sovereign and
rational free will as libertarians assume.
Furthermore, these potentialities appear to be
grounded quite unevenly in our nature and nurture:
human possibilities emerge from and operate
elusively and fragilely within that same formidable
context of heredity and environment which we saw in
the case of human rationality.

At the same time, we must strike a balance as in
the case of rationality. If human potentiality is
elusive within the fabric of human existence, it is
nevertheless a source of creativity and novelty in
human life. As in the case of critical reason,
persons deserve to be appealed to in ways that do

not deny but rather affirm and elicit their always-somewhat-surprising possibilities. We must nevertheless face and deal with the fact that these possibilities are hiddenly mixed with and dominated by the biological and social determinants of the human condition.

Libertarians such as Rothbard curiously combine devastating criticism of the follies and perversities of human history with a remarkable optimism about essential human nature and the possibilities of building a libertarian society. It scarcely seems to occur to them to wonder why, if we are such nobly rational animals, we have so consistently and almost unanimously behaved in such outrageously sheeplike and irrational ways. Committed as they are to describing human groups simply as collections of individuals and to rejecting all abstract and "mystical" notions of "state" or "government" or "society," libertarians in theory at least have no one to blame for the perversities of history but individual human beings themselves.

Yet libertarians leave us with an inexplicable gap between the individual rational animal and the corporate craziness that permeates the human drama. They fall into talking about government and various forms of social organization and institutionalization as a kind of abstract "them" over against rational, productive "us." Why states and churches and various other social institutions and their mythologies have tyrannized over rational individuals from time immemorial is the glaring question libertarians leave unanswered. Their problem is that if they were to grant (as they should) that the grotesqueries of history are rooted deeply in human nature itself, then they would have to concede that homo sapiens is neither free nor rational enough to live in a libertarian world where everything is governed only by free exchange of goods and services. They would have to grant that power-seeking on the one hand and easy subservience on the other are constants of the human conditon. They might even have to admit that, given the dual reality of our marvellous human potentialities and our tragic human limitations, at least some kinds of government may have a positive as well as negative

78

role to play as a terribly imperfect but needed check on the injustices arising from this peculiar mix of creativity and bondage.

Enter the liberal--or at least my liberal. For me the distinctive contribution and strength of twentieth-century liberalism at its best lies in the uniting of passionate commitment to human potentialities with a realistic assessment of human limitations.⁵ Liberalism is more adequate than libertarianism because it takes a more sober view of those aspects of human nature that determine the way we choose and reason and recognizes the need for safeguards against their undesireable manifestations, while at the same time devoting itself to creating conditions that make for the broad realization of our possibilities as human beings.

That, so far as I am concerned, is the sum total of the liberal "creed." That is what I want boldly to call the essence of liberalism or "essential" liberalism. It is a somewhat sloppy social and political perspective, utterly lacking in the crisp consistency of libertarianism, but I believe it understands more deeply our very sloppy world. Very crucially, "essential" liberalism entails no one particular mode of practical application more than another. It does not intrinsically yield "big" federal government, "strong" presidents, bulging bureaucracies, high taxes, or international adventurism and moral crusading. In its practice liberalism is--or certainly ought to be--really and truly pragmatic, in the best moral sense: In its concern to safeguard human liberties, balance competing interests, and make possible the fulfilling of more human potentialities, an "essential" liberalism is not committed in advance to particular programs and policies. It is open to consider whatever are the most effective ones in specific situations.

Let me make it quite clear that what I am calling "essential" liberalism has nothing to do with statism. Quite the contrary: it is precisely a full political commitment to human rights and possibilities that demands the most fundamental skepticism about what government is and what it can do. I agree with the philosophical anarchist Robert Paul Wolff that the only healthy stance toward the state--any state--is irreverently to demythologize its claims and promises and vigorously to protest any and every failure on its part to respect human beings.[6] The sole justification of the state lies in its protection and strengthening of human rights to life, liberty, the pursuit of happiness, and equal justice. Government is simply one pragmatic instrument among others that we must use to secure human welfare. It is a very flawed one at best, and when it is anything more it is usually a menace.

Ideally, the liberalism I envisage should be able to learn from libertarian, conservative, and socialist alike in its ad hoc and situational quest for the best implementation of a "humane realism."[7] It is not intrinsically wedded to the stereotypically "liberal" beliefs that government should be the usual agent of social change, the new is invariably better than the old, businesspersons are the enemy, and people usually don't know what's good for them. But by the same token, of course, neither is an "essential" liberalism bound to the libertarian's a priori insistence that coercion for the sake of social justice is never necessary or desirable or that governmental involvement in human life is always evil. Nor is it tied to conservative veneration of traditional mores or to socialist total planning.

The liberal stands--or certainly should stand-- together with the libertarian in defending and working for maximum personal liberty in terms of private relationships, activities that do not harm other persons, civil rights and liberties, and some measure of participation in social and political decisions that directly affect one's destiny. "My" liberal's concern to safeguard and expand human rights and liberties arises at bottom from her or his devotion to human dignity and potentiality, which she or he considers to be best served by encouraging personal responsibility. Such a liberal believes that individuals should have the maximum liberty to actualize their possibilities consistent with the liberty of other individuals.

80

The libertarian heartily agrees with that last statement, but libertarian and "essential" liberal disagree significantly over the interpretation of "consistent with the freedom of other individuals." Their disagreement clearly reveals their differing assessments of human freedom and rationality. The liberal believes the libertarian rationalist to be remarkably naive in some of her or his most fundamental and important views on this point. For example, libertarians define non-aggression by one individual or group against another strictly in physical terms: No person or group has the right to initiate physical force against any other person or group. Consistent with their belief in the sovereignty of freedom and rationality, they utterly neglect the many and devastating ways in which we inflict psychological, social, and economic violence on one another in the form of injustices such as discrimination and exploitation. Subtle and complex as the area of non-physical aggression is, "my" liberal believes we must face up to its power over our lives and build social and political safeguards against it. Practicing liberals have doubtless made many and tragic mistakes when in positions of political power in trying to construct checks against non-physical violence, and on specific aspects of the problem libertarians may genuinely be right in calling for no meddling at all rather than the disastrous meddling that has often taken place. But improvement will come on the whole through wise social and political safeguards as opposed to stupid or ignorant ones--not through no safeguards at all.

The central pillar of applied libertarianism is an entire society built on the model of laissez-faire capitalism or an absolutely free market of goods and services. Here it is that an "essential" liberalism finds libertarian rationalism massively exceeding the bounds of good sense. The whole idea sounds wonderful, but it really is u-topian: it applies to no place, past, present, or future. The root dilemma is that human beings are simply not rational enough for an absolutely free market society to be a just one. To put it another way, because it is a human enterprise the free market contains the seeds of its own corruption. One might have thought that libertarians would have learned more than they seem to have from the actual history of capitalism in England and the United States. (Not that the market was ever totally free, but it certainly enjoyed far fewer controls in the nineteenth and early twentieth centuries than it does today.)

Precisely because human beings--including businesspersons and industrialists--are not the rational animals libertarians think we are, the free market corrupts itself out of being free. As Wolff aptly observes, "reliance on the market is fundamentally irrational once men know how to control it in order to avoid its undesired consequences."[8] Individuals and organizations who become powerful through the dynamics of the free market try to use their power to make the market unfree--and often they have succeeded. Others band together to restrict the market by fixing prices and driving competition out of business. Thus we have monopolies and cartels and multi-national corporations. The apparent libertarian belief that persons interested in economic power have no interest in political power is another conviction which is belied by the evidence. Some businesspersons and industrialists have always tried to manipulate what governmental power and money there was in their favor, from the nineteenth-century railroad barons to General Motors and ITT. It is probably safe to say that if there had been no state--the anarchist libertarian's dream--powerful economic interests would have invented one.

The further libertarian conviction that producers simply satisfy consumer wants and meet consumer demands reveals an amazing lack of insight into the complexities of psyche and society. To quote James Thurber's correction of Lincoln's famous statement, "You can fool [or otherwise victimize] too many of the people too much of the time"--and get by with it even on the free market. Then of course there is international free trade--an excellent principle which is adhered to by "capitalists" just about as long as it takes for their product to start to feel the pinch of foreign competition.

I am not "picking on" the world of commerce and industry. It is simply that this is the libertarian model for social and political thinking, and I wish to point out that businesspersons manifest the same sorts of irrationalities as the rest of us. In point of fact, I believe that an economy which is free in a manner that is consistent with the liberty of the whole society of individual human beings is a healthy and vital aspect of that liberty. It is just that a purely laissez-faire economy can never be that, but only one that is regulated humanely and justly. If the principle of laissez-faire is too rational for us poor mortals in the economic arena, it follows that its application to areas of life in which there is even more non-rational investment-- law, police protection, defense, government and politics, education--is doomed to failure. Human beings are simply not up to it.

Libertarians typically reduce the concept of the coercive authority of government to that of physical force; one favorite image of governmental authority is the gun. An unlikely bedfellow, Mao Tse-tung, said something very similar: "Power grows out of the barrel of a gun." I mention Mao's famous aphorism because the philosopher Hannah Arendt, taking off from this saying, argues persuasively in her book On Violence that political authority is something much more complex than sheer physical power.[9] Among other factors, there is virtually always a crucial element of at least minimal voluntary assent on which any government that wants to be anything other than a totalitarian reign of terror must depend.

It is entirely conceivable to me that we might develop in the United States (Britain, the Scandinavian countries, and Holland have something approximating it), through the continued reform of our present institutions, a political order the coercive powers of which could be symbolized by a gun only in a highly forced and simplistic manner. I have in mind such actual and possible changes as the abolition of the draft; the strengthening and enforcing of laws guaranteeing individual rights, liberties, and opportunities regardless of sex, race, political or religious beliefs, or ethnic background; strong safeguards of individual

83

citizens' rights over against governmental authority
and invasion of privacy; the abolition of the
present penal system in favor of the principles of
restitution to the victim and community-based
rehabilitation; the repeal of abortion laws and laws
governing sexual activity among consenting adults;
reform of campaign financing and governmental
operation; balanced environmental legislation and
practices; effective Congressional control over
warmaking; and radical welfare and tax reform which
would be generally seen to be fair by all economic
levels of society. Now this would still not be the
kind of political order the libertarians want. But
I suggest that progress in these and other areas
would minimize physical coercion and maximize
citizen assent to such a degree that the image of
the gun would be highly inappropriate.

I suggest further that such reforms and others
reveal just those positive and (the liberal
believes) necessary functions government has to play
in protecting and enhancing human liberty. And this
of course brings us back to my fundamental
philosophical disagreement with libertarianism:
our interpretation of human behavior. I observe
human beings to be both self-regarding and other-
regarding, with a significant measure of
irrationality in both forms of behavior. We tend
toward selfishness rather than healthy self-regard,
with all the exploiting and hurting of others that
that produces; while our altruism has a bent in the
direction of unthinking devotion to nations,
religions, and other causes. I want to emphasize
and affirm again the vital importance of reason; it
is just that I must also recognize, as a matter of
description, that reason struggles against
formidable pushes in the other direction.

Because of these behavioral propensities, I
believe that government must be more than simply a
system of laws, police, and courts. It must be more
precisely for the sake of individual liberty. I do
not see how liberty can be adequately defined as the
individual's absolute right to his or her life and
property when, human irrationality being what it is,
other individuals are thereby exploited or deprived
or otherwise suffer as a result. For individual

84

liberty cannot be adequately conceived apart from the general liberty of others, from the common weal. Freedom from deprivation of opportunity through discrimination and exploitation by the irrationalities of others is an essential element of liberty. To describe the migrant worker, the Appalachian miner, or the black ghetto dweller as "free" simply insofar as they are not physically harmed by others and in some wildly abstract way can "do what they want" with their life and property, strikes me as little more than a bad joke. The struggle for educational, economic, and legal equality by no means entails a "levelling out" of real human distinctions and abilities. It is a struggle for a social order which is both more humane and more free for a greater number of individuals with all their variety and differences. The alleviation of grinding poverty, of sex, race, and ethnic discrimination, of educational disadvantages, of bad living conditions--all those things enhance my liberty by enhancing it for more people. Many whites and males have discovered the truth of this through their own experience of the black and women's movements.

Government has a positive role to play in "promoting the general welfare": in protecting us from one another's selfishness, in actively helping to alleviate the human condition, and in promoting the greatest liberty for the greatest number. Government sometimes does a good job of this, and sometimes a bad job. But the task is to rectify the bad jobs and improve the good, not to abolish the function altogether. As I have said, it genuinely may be that in certain areas present and possible agencies of the private sector can and could do part of the job more efficiently and humanely. It is definitely true that citizen organization and agitation around various issues, private benevolent and educational organizations, and media exposure are vitally important agents of social liberty and justice in a democratic society. But they cannot do everything. In many instances government alone has the money, the organization, and the legal authority to correct injustices and enhance liberty on the large scale needed in a modern, complex nation-state. As for a purely economic issue such as postal service, if private enterprise can do that job more cheaply and efficiently, a truly pragmatic liberalism has no stake in perpetuating it as a government function so long as all persons are truly and equitably provided service by a private postal system.

The case of the partial alleviation during recent years of black Americans' victimization by whites illustrates concretely my inability to accept libertarianism. I fail to see how, in a libertarian society, blacks would be any better off today than they were twenty years ago. In a libertarian society there would be no fair employment, fair housing, or fair education laws. There would not be the active weight of official governmental support and sanctions in redressing the legal, social, educational, and economic injustices against blacks. As I understand the conception of a libertarian society, its obligations would be at an end as long as discrimination was not officially permitted in public institutions, what laws there were were applied and enforced equally, and black persons were not physically threatened.

The example of injustices against black Americans also illustrates the fact that social mores are a far more pervasive and powerful force making for concrete lack of liberty than is government. Libertarians persist in making government the chief villain, while exhibiting what seems to me to be a real blind side with respect to the deep-rooted irrationalities of social existence. As racial minority groups, women, and young people with different coiffures and life-styles can testify even at the present time, repressive laws are not needed to keep people down. Repressive laws, it is true, can institutionalize and reinforce the stranglehold of social conformity. But by the same token, just laws strictly enforced can be one important agent among others in loosening up social strictures.

I should add that the irrationalities surrounding our altruistic behavior also require checks built into the system of government. In some ways this is more difficult, since of course political institutions are functions of the nation-

86

state, which perpetually tends to absolutize and aggrandize itself. Yet even here the task is revision, not abolition. In this area laws and enlightened legal interpretation probably represent the most effective use of government. I have in mind the legal recognition of the individual's rights over against the government, as in such cases as Bill of Rights guarantees, protection against massive government data files and spying on citizens, and newspersons' immunity from subpoena of their sources. Such laws represent one of the highest and most desireable achievements of democratic government.

Let me face frankly the issue of governmental coercion which libertarians raise so urgently. I believe liberals should be perfectly candid about this. Of course certain forms of governmental coercion are legitimate for the sake of the protection and enhancement of indvidual liberty. Conservatives, libertarians, liberals, and socialists all believe in some degree of political coercion; the issue is not coercion versus non-coercion. For the liberal the task is the wise use of only those sorts of coercion required to alleviate human deprivation and lack of opportunity, to rectify injustices, and to protect the life and property of persons. Taxation and legislation for such purposes is coercive for the sake of the greatest liberty for the greatest number; it is designed to counteract all those other sorts of coercion which human irrationality imposes on us in the way of discrimination and exploitation. For governmental coercion is only one of a number of sorts of coercion in human society, and libertarians once again appear to me to neglect all those ways in which we coerce one another quite apart from the machinery of the state. A libertarian society would simply be one which would eliminate certain forms of coercion, allow others to continue, and as I see it end up exacerbating the latter. Specifically, a libertarian society would seem to me to be one in which individuals would be even more at the mercy of coercion by the acquisitive mentality, economic power, and local prejudice than they are now.

Am I trying to impose my values on society when I support, for example, legislation and programs

87

which tax all of us for the sake of remedying injustices and alleviating lack of opportunity for some of us? Of course I am--and I think liberals should be perfectly candid about this too. But the fact is that all interested parties have a vision of society "made in their image," which some of them work to get most of their fellow citizens to accept. This is no less true of libertarians than of liberals, and let us have no self-deception on that score. Ostensibly the libertarian's laissez-faire society where everyone goes her or his own way is a "no-imposition" model. Actually, it is a model which, because of human irrationality, the liberal fears will permit the imposition of injustices and deprivations and a particular image of human being on far too many people. Happily, in a democratic society both the libertarian and the liberal must simply try to persuade their fellow citizens of the superiority of their vision of society, and let them accept or reject it. I think that in the long run the liberal is as confident that people will see the superiority of a concept of liberty that is both individual and social, as the libertarian is that they will prefer his or her purely individual notion of liberty.

I cannot share the typical libertarian rhetoric about the specter of Big Brother and 1984. 1984 will not be created by Keynesian economics, New Dealism, or democratic socialism. 1984's happen when groups with totalitarian mentalities manage in one way or another to take over a country. The resistance of a people to that sort of thing is the result of their commitment to liberty and the viability of their institutions as protectors and enhancers of liberty. It has nothing intrinsically to do with being Keynesian or Friedmanian, Democrat or Republican or Libertarian. It is not the principle of the responsibility of all citizens for protecting and enhancing the liberty of all through taxation, laws, and social programs that is the threat to liberty. It is rather things like governmental unaccountability, secrecy, contempt for individual rights and privacy, self-aggrandizement, and captivity to powerful economic interests that are the real dangers.

The libertarian affirmation of individual human dignity, freedom, and rationality is a refreshing and urgently needed voice from what is for the liberal a new and unexpected part of the political spectrum. The passionate defense of individual rights and liberties by Rothbard and other libertarians, and their vigilant criticisms of governmental arrogance and corruption, should be welcomed by liberals on most counts. But the liberal I have described in turn needs to remind the libertarian that her or his principles and practices emphasize only one side of human nature--our noble endowment as possessors of a unique measure of potentiality and reason--and underplay the bondages and irrationalities resulting from our formidable natural and social limitations. In its admittedly muddled way "essential" liberalism tries to do justice to the whole muddled mix of human potentialities and limitations that produces the ambiguities, distortions, and tragedies of human history. Out of this "humane realism" comes the liberal belief that laissez-faire is not a possible state of human society; that human rights and possibilities require an active offsetting of human irrationalities. The human being portrayed by libertarianism seems to be all grandeur and no misery, all Eden and no Fall. Such angelism produces a social and political theory full of noble sentiment but lacking in depth and possibility.

[1]N.Y : Macmillan, 1973.

[2]P. 40.

[3]Throughout this essay I shall arbitrarily use the word "liberty" to indicate freedom in the political and economic senses, in order to distinguish it from freedom in the metaphysical sense of "free will"; for the latter I shall use the term "freedom." When I must use the adjectival form "free", the noun it modifies should adequately indicate which sense of the term is intended.

[4] The Future of an Illusion, trans. & ed. by James Strachey, N.Y.: W. W. Norton, 1961, p. 53.

[5]It is worth pointing out that of course the word "liberalism" used to denote a political philosophy has had a strange history. The liberalism of the nineteenth century, now called "classical liberalism," as expounded for example by John Stuart Mill, was very close to what is now call libertarianism: a strong advocacy of individual liberty and of very limited government as the way to preserve and strengthen it. Liberalism in our time, largely through Roosevelt and the New Deal, has come to mean rather the view that government must play an active and substantial role precisely in order to offset gross inequities and assure the greatest liberty for the greatest number of people.

[6]See especially his In Defense of Anarchism, N.Y.: Harper & Row, 1970. Interestingly, Wolff's own theory seems to me to be vitiated by the same sort of superficial rationalism that I find in libertarianism.

[7]My situational or contextual approach to political liberalism is greatly indebted to the situational theory of ethics of my teacher and friend Joseph Fletcher. See his Situation Ethics, Philadelphia: Westminster, 1966.

[8]In Defense of Anarchism, p. 81.

[9]Harcourt, Brace & World, 1970.

IV.

TWO EARTHLY GRACES

In Christian theology, grace is the "uncalculating,
unlimited, and unconditional" love of God,[1] bestowed
upon us in many and varied ways: in life itself, in
the beauty and sustenance of the natural order, in
knowledge and art, in conscience and community, in
reconciliation and healing, in deliverance from
specific evils, and of course supremely and all-
embracingly in Christ, through whom human beings
receive everlasting fulfillment in union with God
and one another. The power of Christianity's
classical "theologians of grace"--Augustine, Luther,
Calvin, Edwards--lies precisely in the ineffable
grandeur and beauty of their apprehension of deity
as utterly, undeservedly, unexpectedly gracious to
humankind. Their grace-intoxicated vision of
reality was seriously vitiated by their grim
preoccupation with everlasting damnation as our just
punishment for Adam's and Eve's fall, but even that
cannot take away substantively from its depth and
power. Indeed, I have argued elsewhere that a fully
universalized version of the Augustinian
proclamation of radical divine grace is the only
form of the Christian message that speaks with any
power and plausibility to the radical depths of our
human bondage.[2]

To face realistically and knowledgeably our
servitude to suffering and to the dark riddle of our
own natures is to realize that our only health and
hope lie in grace in its varied manifestations. But
this is as true, I maintain, for a secular-
humanistic as it is for a Christian view of life.
Even without God, human existence is rendered
tolerable and made whole only by grace--earthly
rather than heavenly grace, to be sure, but grace
nevertheless. The Augustinian vision of both our
radical brokenness and our healing sola gratia
remains vital to understanding and living even when
demythologized and translated into agnostic terms.

For the essence of grace is its character as sheer gift. All those things in our lives that come to us unbidden and unanticipated, spontaneously and surprisingly, to delight, to alleviate, to enrich, to heal--all those belong to the category of grace. Many of the things that Christianity includes under graces of God are just as surely graces etsi deus non daretur: the extraordinary beauties of nature, loving human relationships of many sorts, active compassion reaching out to our need and suffering, the astonishing expressions of human creativity in the arts, the excitement of learning and discovery. I suggest that it is precisely these graces and others that largely render human existence, so filled with conflict and ambiguity, tolerable and meaningful.

In this essay I want to explore two from among the many earthly graces that merit exploration: compassion and beauty. I do so in the first place because these two graces have been very important in my own existence. I examine them, secondly, because of their relationship to the foundational issues of human bondage and ultimate mystery. As I noted in Chapter One, compassion would appear to be a central element in an ethics arising from a "tragic wisdom" that grasps existentially as well as intellectually the abysmal reality of our suffering. The world's beauty, for its part, functions for many unbelievers as the nearest they can come to divinity, and the ecstasy with which such beauty is often appropriated their closest approach to religious experience.

1. The Moral Grace of Compassion

Compassion comes from the Latin com (with) + pati (to suffer). To be compassionate is to suffer with others, to undergo or experience with them their unhappiness, discomfort, trouble, or pain, with a desire to help. Compassion is linguistically synonymous with the Greek-derived word "sympathy": syn (together) + pathos (suffering); and the two terms are often used interchangeably. A closely-related term used much more freely now than it used to be is "empathy," from the Greek en (in) + pathos (suffering). Empathy is intended to convey a more intense form of compassion than sympathy: in some sense actually projecting oneself into other persons, trying to feel what they are feeling "from within" or put oneself in their place.

Two further refinements need to be introduced immediately. The first is the recognition that identification with others in their sufferings is at best an imperfect activity, since one person cannot literally experience what another person experiences. Compassion requires a certain capacity for feeling directed beyond the self, bound up closely together with an imagination that can transfer analogically back and forth between self and others. These qualities are in different persons in quite varying degrees, and cultural factors can in addition play a large role in conditioning the selection of the objects of people's compassion. The commonest form of cultural shaping of compassion is regarding one's own group--tribe, class, race, nation--as the "natural" objects of sympathy, but not "outsiders." But I tend to think that, with the exception of certain severe pathologies such as autism, no human being is utterly devoid of the affective and imaginative capacity for compassion. It also appears that compassion is more deeply rooted in our individual-social nature than to be accounted for entirely in cultural terms, as seems to be evidenced by the spontaneous ways in which it tends to break down and move beyond cultural barriers of in-group and out-group.

A second needed elaboration is the observation that when I speak of "compassion" I mean active compassion, an identification with the bondage of others that seeks concretely to alleviate and heal. Only active compassion is ethical compassion. It is entirely possible to be acutely sensitive to the many forms of our human suffering but overwhelmed and paralyzed into a passive fatalism or a self-protective cynicism. Indeed, I think we must understand and sympathize with the sorts of personal-environmental experiences and qualities that can drive some persons to that pass most of the time and a great many of us to it at least some of the time. But I am here concerned with ethics, and with the conviction that without compassion that is

active human life would long ago have become utterly
and completely impossible.

In what sense is compassion grace? It is grace
for those who are its recipients. Jesus' parable of
the Good Samaritan (Luke 10:30-35) is a paradigm of
the gracious character of compassion. The Samaritan
"was moved to pity" (NEB translation) for the beaten
man. The Greek word is the vivid and graphic ἐσ-
πλαγχνίσθη, from τὰ σπλάγχνα: viscera, inward
parts, bowels. Compassion here is as it were
"feeling in one's guts" for another. The
compassionate Samaritan tends to the unfortunate
victim's wounds, takes him to an inn where he takes
care of him, then pays the innkeeper to continue his
care. For the traveller who had been mugged and
robbed the Samaritan's appearance and acts of mercy
were sheer grace: unexpected caring and healing in
a situation of great need and pain.

Some acts of compassion toward us are dramatic,
like those of the Good Samaritan; many are more
commonplace but still have the character of grace.
Times of war bring out the most bestial in humans;
they are also filled with countless deeds of
compassion, elicited by the many forms of suffering
that are the consequences of war. On the far
quieter quotidian level where most of us live out
our lives, compassionate acts are just as essential
and gracious to the recipients. Time and again my
own undramatic life has been graced by the active
sympathy of others toward my need or distress:
sickness, an operation, the sad ending of a
relationship, anxieties about my children,
professional disappointment, periodic bouts of
Weltschmerz. I think, too, of the varied
compassionate ones and the varied forms of their
compassion. The flower and card from my wife that
dispelled or lightened my gloom and her repeated
support amid my frustrations; the active
availability of a friend, patiently listening to me
spill out my problem and being there for and with
me; the concern of a complete stranger who stops to
help me when I am stranded on the highway; the
kindness of neighbors coming to my aid in a number
of often surprising ways--what are all these but
graces that in small and large ways "light up my
life"?

I have said that I am using compassion in the sense of ethical--that is, active--compassion. Compassion is the essential dimension of grace in the moral sphere; but it is by no means the whole of ethics. Ethics involves general value appraisal and examining specific issues and situations in its light; recognition of duties or obligations; weighing of alternative courses of actions; consideration of ends sought, means to their realization, and possible or probable consequences. These are all activities of moral reasoning, and they clearly transcend compassion. Sympathy or empathy alone is nowhere nearly enough to make shift for the whole work of ethics. Compassion alone can sometimes act ignorantly and harmfully; compassion alone cannot deal adequately with the complexity of many moral issues, with problems of justice and fairness, with ends and means and consequences.

But while compassion is clearly only one element in the totality that is the moral life, I want to argue that it is an absolutely essential element both in the foundation and in the implementation of the moral life. Without the compassion that is a "natural" quality at the very roots of human moral experience and its continued presence in moral judgments and actions, the business of ethics would be harsh, rigid, formal, dessicated, impersonal. Compassion is the affective dimension, the "heart" of the moral life, which must be present together with the "head" of moral reasoning to create moral wholeness among persons.

Compassion plainly seems to be a central affective element among the factors that give rise to the moral life. However we may wish to account for it biologically and psychologically, sympathy is one expression of human fellow-feeling: all those primary ways in which humans recognize and experience one another as beings like themselves. Fellow-feeling manifests itself in the various forms of sexual and social bonding without which there would be no such thing as social existence. It expresses itself in mating and parenting, in language and celebration and rules, in tribe and lodge and other social groupings.

One of the foundational moral articulations of fellow-feeling is compassion, our imaginative identification with the suffering of others issuing in a desire to help them. People tend spontaneously to respond with pity even to the suffering of non-human animals. The wounded, helpless fawn or dog elicits our compassion as fellow-creatures who also have experienced pain and helplessness. In the case of other human beings in need or distress the recognition of them as fellow-creatures is of course more direct. At the same time, on the inter-human level we find a paradox produced by the very large role played by culture in shaping our behavior. The paradox is that although biologically we should have the closest fellow-feeling with the other members of our own species, culturally we are often conditioned to regard persons outside our own group as aliens or enemies.

Yet as I have suggested, the spontaneity of compassionate fellow-feeling has a way in all sorts of different circumstances of breaking through the cultural barriers imposed by notions of "us" and "them." Despite the overwhelming degree to which most Germans and Poles were conditioned during the Nazi era to despise and regard as sub-human all Jews, there are numerous examples of individuals and families having compassion on Jews at great risk to themselves. In all cases such as these we must of course recognize that there are positive <u>cultural</u> forces at work--for example, the Christian ethics of neighbor-love--countering the negative moulding by certain other cultural factors such as the Nazi propaganda that played on centuries of Christian antisemitism. But my own view would be that various universal ethical principles, such as those of the major religions enjoining compassion toward all persons, build on and reinforce culturally that fellow-feeling that is rooted in our evolutionary history and biological nature as <u>homo</u> <u>sapiens</u>.

Of interest to me in considering the role of compassion in the moral life is its importance as an ingredient in moral decisions and moral character. A philosophy colleague of mine has told me of leading a discussion at the end of the semester in an introductory ethics class that I find illuminating on this point. After the members of the class had spent the semester reading and discussing the classical ethical theorists and their theories--Plato, Aristotle, Kant, Mill, Nietzsche-- she posed to them the question, What sorts of persons would you most like to live in community with? Would you prefer utilitarians, Kantians, Aristotelians, or what? My colleague was struck by the fact that her students emerged from the discussion preferring to live with what might best be described as liberal Christians; at the other end of the spectrum, they were completely "turned off" by the prospect of living with persons who really took seriously Kant's approach to ethics. The instructor, a childhood Episcopalian who is now a complete agnostic with very little interest in religion, was intrigued because her class' collective judgment coincided with her own privately-held view of the matter.

Why did the members of the class prefer to live in community with liberal-minded Christians? (By "liberal" and "liberal-minded" I do not mean to refer to theological liberalism but to liberality of spirit: the opposite of narrow, rigid, dogmatic, puritanical, self-righteous, obsessive, hidebound.) Their preference had nothing really to do with Christian theology and everything to do with a certain notion of concrete, living ethics. The class believed that such persons were more likely to display certain virtues that they regarded as indispensable to life in community: honesty, integrity, trustworthiness, openness, flexibility. Above all--and bound up with and pervading the other virtues--I think the class placed a very high value on caring, sensitivity, understanding, and compassion among humans, and believed at least that they would find them best exemplified by persons who were personally moulded by a familiar religious tradition that also places a very great value on those expressions of fellow-feeling. They believed that such persons could be trusted to make truly humane moral decisions: decisions not only informed by good moral reasoning but also flexibly sensitive to concrete human needs and situations. Whether the class articulated it specifically or not, what they thought they saw in such persons was a moral wholeness that unites head and heart, reason and feeling, principle and intuition. Compassion is an

98

essential element in the affective side of that
wholeness: that caring and sensitivity toward
others that reaches out to them in their need and
trouble and pain.

The point of this example has not been to make a
case for Christianity or Christian ethics. It has
not been to argue whether liberal-minded Christians
are on the whole really that way or not (although
the ethics students clearly perceived at least some
they had known as that sort of person). Obviously
there are humanists, Jews, Buddhists--people of
various religions and none--who admirably manifest
the moral qualities the class desired, and many
Christians who do not. "Liberal Christian" was a
moral type familiar to the students, one they could
in some way concretely work with. (I should add
that a common religious phenomenon of our day is the
ex-Christian who continues to be profoundly moulded
by Christian moral values after leaving the church.
Typical is the lapsed minister or priest who is now
actively involved in mental health and other helping
professions. Such persons continue in an important
sense to be "liberal Christians.") For myself, the
example raises the important issue of the value of a
religiously-based ethics, as opposed to a purely
secular ethics, in encouraging precisely those
affective elements epitomized in compassion that I
believe are so essential to wholeness in the moral
life; but that is an issue I cannot pursue here.[3]

The judgment of the ethics class, my colleague
and I agree, is one that has been borne out in our
own experience. I am comfortable placing my trust
in persons whose moral decisions are permeated by a
rich humane feeling-sensitivity toward real persons
in real situations. By contrast, I have an almost
instinctive distrust of ethical rationalists,
persons who attempt to deal with moral issues solely
on the basis of principles and reasoning. They seem
to me often to exhibit that moral purblindness
nicely summed up by the father in The Rainmaker who
told his son that "you're so full of what's right
you can't see what's good."[4] Immanuel Kant, who
contributed so many valuable perceptions to the
analysis of ethics, was led by his own rigorous
formalistic moral theory into judgments that were
examples par excellence of this purblindness. No

wonder my colleague's students thought that living
with Kantians would be especially unattractive!

I read and listen to philosophical arguments
about current ethical issues that are sometimes
marked by a strangely dehumanized vocabulary, by an
abstractedness, by the curious absence of what would
seem to be an essential dimension of ethical
discussion. Some philosophical arguments against
abortion, for example, seem to me quite chilling in
their relentless logic and their utter ignoring of
the flesh-and-blood reality of human frailty and
desperation, women's experience, unloved children,
discrimination against the poor, and the ugly
personal and social consequences of making abortion
illegal. I believe that only persons who deal with
such matters from out of the ethical wholeness in
which concrete compassion for other humans is
dominant can be trusted to talk sense and not
nonsense, to make wise rather than truncated moral
decisions. To those who are the recipients of such
compassion it bears the marks of grace rather than
of law.

Obviously possessing the quality of humane
sensitivity does not protect us from mistakes--
sometimes bad ones--in moral decision-making. But
ethical rationalists, I have observed, are often
involved in the worst sort of mistake in ethics:
self-deception. The person who tries to be
rigorously rational about ethics (or, indeed, about
life generally) is precisely a person who is likely
to deceive herself or himself about her or his own
passions and prejudices. Suppressing or attempting
to ignore one's intuitions and feelings too easily
involves repression; reasoning becomes
rationalization; self-ignorance takes its hidden
revenge in unfortunate ways. To be sure, the person
who tries to be holistic and concretely sensitive is
also liable to a kind of self-deception: believing
that sentiment or "heart" or sufficient compassion
is enough to do the whole job of caring responsibly
for others. But to err on the side of fellow-
feeling seems to me to be a much less dangerous and
more readily correctable sort of mistake than to err
on the side of a blinkered reasoning.

Taking into account the intuitive deliverances of our fellow-feeling also makes the business of ethics somewhat sloppy and contextual rather than tidy and principled. But that is only to say that it brings ethics into a closer and more natural relationship with human life, which is after all very sloppy and complicated and asymmetrical. Reasoning is crucially important in the moral life, and there can be no ethical wholeness without it. But our ability to illuminate and understand something of the complexities of moral existence with reason is not the same thing as a rationalism that ignores feelings and reduces complexities.

The affective dimension of fellow-feeling, then, is essential to moral wholeness and moral character; and compassion is one of its highest expression. But of course our capacities for fellow-feeling generally and compassion specifically vary greatly, and in addition they must be developed and cultivated in order to become ethically mature. What our genetic endowment precisely contributes to our characterological possibilities we do not yet know very much about. But we know a great deal about what habitual parental indifference, rejection, hostility, and abuse can do to develop distrust, suspicion, anger, and hatred (of self and others) rather than fellow-feeling in their children. Conversely, the child who is given physical and emotional warmth and security from the beginning is much more likely to actualize her or his potentialities for feeling with and caring about other persons. What is more, even the person who by the grace of nature and nurture has strong and spontaneous resources of compassion must as she or he matures cultivate a truly ethical compassion through intelligence and will; and that is the difficult and always unfinished task of a lifetime. The wide range of our capacities for compassion should of course make those of us who are capable of sympathetic understanding of that fact compassionate in turn toward those whose fellow-feeling has been arrested or smothered, while at the same time seeking to elicit and help cultivate what affective possibilities lie hidden within them.

But how desperately all of us--those who are blessed with great-heartedness equally with those

who are not--need to be treated compassionately!
What an unthinkably cruel nightmare life would be
(and is for some) without its grace bestowed on us!
For the strongest of us are at the same time so
frail, the most integrated so inwardly legion, the
most independent so in need of help, the most
feeling so insensitive, the sanest so confused. And
of course there is the ubiquitous fact of suffering,
in its many physical and mental forms, which all of
us experience in greater or lesser degree and many
in such bewilderingly disproportionate measure.
Sacramentally, the word of forgiveness and comfort
and the act of succour and mercy body forth in the
midst of our bondage to heal and to save. In its
many voices Miserere me is the universal cry of
human need and suffering; in its many-faceted
language and deeds compassion is the universally
gracious response to that cry.

2. The Religious Experience of Beauty

Immanuel Kant stated that the only thing that is
unqualifiedly good is the moral good will. What
Freud and other depth psychologists have since
taught us of the ambiguity and self-deception in
human willing has rendered Kant's judgment dubious.
As a less problematic candidate for the
unqualifiedly good I propose beauty. A person for
whom beauty in both its natural and its human forms
is a personal necessity for living and sanity, I am
continually struck by the forceful impression that
within a human world enmeshed in bondage and riddled
with ambiguity beauty alone stands out as
intrinsically whole and not in need of
justification. In its wonder and purity earthly
beauty is a profound source of ecstasy and
consolation.

It is hardly an exaggeration to say that for
many persons who for whatever reason must live their
lives without religious faith and the divine, beauty
is a God-surrogate. As a source of ecstasy it takes
us out of ourselves into a realm of enjoyment and
even sublimity that is timeless, a "little
eternity." In so doing beauty also functions as an
ever-fresh source of solace, healing, and renewal
amid a world of riddles, frustration, and pain. As

a creator of ecstasy and healing, beauty is clearly one of the graces in our existence--for some, the highest and holiest and most mysteriously transcendent of graces.

Grace abounds in all forms of beauty, human-created and natural. By "human" or "human-created" beauty I have in mind those wonderfully rich and varied expressions we call the arts. In music, in painting, in poetry and fiction we clearly recognize uniquely human artifacts; to draw on the etymology of the word poetry, they are things that are made or produced (Gr. poieo = to make, produce, execute, especially works of art). Thus the distinction between human and natural expressions of beauty would seem to be straightforward: the former are produced by human beings, the latter are not.

But certain qualifications need to be made. For what we call "nature" has been extensively revised and developed by human beings. A very great part of what an urban dweller like me enjoys as "nature" on a day-to-day basis is the product of substantial human "interference" with nature extending back often through many generations; and even the rural inhabitant--for example, the farmer--lives to a striking degree within this human-altered physical environment.

To cite my own daily experience of nature as an example: When the town of Lawrence was first settled in 1854 the area was almost entirely devoid of trees except along the banks of the Kansas River where the earliest houses and stores were built. The University of Kansas was founded in 1866 and located atop the most prominent hill in the area, which was utterly bare of any vegetation except for prairie grass. Over many years citizens of the town and members of the university community--with that traditional sense of responsibility to leave a heritage for generations they would never live to see, a sense which sadly has become very attenuated in our day of instant production and gratification--planted trees and shrubs of every sort all over the town and the campus. Today, of course, the area is totally different from what it was one hundred years ago even from the standpoint of "nature" alone. The university campus, regarded widely by vistors as one

103

of the loveliest large campuses in the United States, abounds in trees and shrubs of great variety and carefully designed flower gardens, all immaculately cared for within an overall plan supervised by a landscape architect and his staff. In my day-to-day existence it is chiefly the "natural" beauties of the university campus, together with those of the town that spreads out all around the base of Mt. Oread and the surrounding countryside, that are my ever-renewing matins and vespers and communion.

Thus human art plays a very great role in much of what we call "nature." There is of course a great deal of natural beauty in the world that is still very largely in its wild state--many mountains and waterfalls and flora and fauna in protected or uncharted areas--although I suspect that many vacationers in, say, our national parks would be surprised to learn how considerable the human "tampering" with the natural environment has been precisely in order to render it not only more humanly accessible (consider all the convenient "nature trails") but also more beautiful. I remember hiking in the Great Smokies and coming upon a plaque indicating that the whole magnificent area I was in had been devastated by fire in the 1930's and extensively replanted in order to look "wildly" beautiful as it did when I was there forty years later.

At the same time, we commonly and I think rightly distinguish between even a planted tree and a poem. The former is still clearly "nature" in the sense of being part of the natural order; in the case of the tree, a non-human living organism in a setting of sky and grass. Human-altered natural objects are also much less obviously "made" than works of art. Their raw material is typically much more prominent than the human form imposed on them. There is usually much less artistic control because of the very "nature" of the natural object and our human intentions regarding it. In the case of living organisms this results from the vagaries of cellular division and growth, and in the case of inorganic natural objects such as mountains and waterfalls from a human concern to interfere as little as is necessary with their natural state. In addition, there is often an astonishing aesthetic complexity and variety in natural beauty--the formations of the rock crystals, the delicate shades of color in a flower, the endless species of sea animals--that is all the more wonder-ful because it is so obviously not produced (although it may in some instances be considerably enhanced) by human beings but is simply among the "givens" of the world.

By contrast, poetry is much more obviously a human creation in both its matter and its form. So are painting, sculpture (even when part of the stone is left rough), music, architecture, drama, and the other art forms. In this realm the raw materials used--stone, wood and other organic products, metal--are characteristically transformed into a state far different from their natural state: they become, for example, musical instruments, printed pages, paints and dyes on canvas and other sorts of cloth, steel and bronze castings. These human objects also often appear in artificial settings: theaters, concert halls, museums, homes. They are characteristically non-natural in obvious ways that set them sharply apart from natural objects and the natural environment. The painting is strikingly different from even the artistically cultivated flower garden, the symphony from the beautiful sounds in the carefully maintained bird sanctuary.

Thus we can make a distinction, although not a sharp one, between human art and what we call natural beauty. (I have used adverbs such as "typically," "usually," and "characteristically" to indicate that there are exceptions to virtually every distinction I have made between natural and human forms of beauty.) Furthermore, many persons definitely prefer one mode of beauty over the other. For some, like William Wordsworth, the beauty of nature possesses a wonder and a holiness that no human art can possibly attain. For others--perhaps a Saul Bellow or a Leonard Bernstein--the marvel and the mystery of human creativity are in the foreground. Many, like myself, are unable to say that they experience the grace of beauty in one mode more than in the other. In my own experience of nature it has been chiefly the modest beauties of my own locale that I mentioned earlier, the seasonally-changing trees and gentle hills that are my daily environment, rather than the more spectacular sights of the Rockies or the California coast, that have nourished and renewed me. But I am no less graced by artistic beauty, most powerfully by music, poetry, and fiction, but also by drama, dance, painting, and sculpture.

But these varieties of the experience of beauty are a many-splendored richness and not a problem to be sorted out within the perspective from which I am examining beauty. For as I indicated at the beginning of this essay, I am interested in beauty in all its forms just insofar as it functions for human beings as grace: as a source of ecstasy, ennoblement, consolation, healing, renewal, peace. My focus is in a sense a "theological" one, in a manner analogous to Paul Tillich's proposal that theology examines the various facets of human culture--for example, the arts--only insofar as they are expressions of "ultimate concern."[5] The difference is one of what Tillich called "formal criteria": He focussed on modes of beauty as manifestations of the things that concern us ultimately; my preoccupation is with beauty as the multifaceted source of qualities of human experience that are recognizably "religious" in character.

The delimited and purely functional perspective I am adopting not only embraces unproblematically both human and natural forms of beauty; it also, as I have hinted, avoids the aesthetic problem of the great variety and differences among people's perceptions and evaluations of beauty generally. Obviously from culture to culture, epoch to epoch, and individual to individual there can be considerable difference in aesthetic standards and judgments as well as flat contradiction. The music of India sounds amorphous, directionless, tedious to many Westerners; the elegant music of Haydn, so celebrated in the late eighteenth century, was eclipsed for many years and only quite recently revived; the music of Schoenberg and Cage can arouse passionate controversy. But all these are issues-- and important ones--for aesthetics. The only issue relevant to a discussion of beauty as an earthly grace is the various functions that experiences of what the experiencers want to call the beautiful play in their lives. It may be objected that by focussing on beauty only as a source of grace in human experience I am no longer really talking about experience of the beautiful but experience of the holy. In other words, when beauty is a source of ecstasy, consolation, and healing it is no longer being experienced as beauty but rather as a religious object. But I do not think this is the case. The truth of the matter, I believe, is that the experience of objects as "beautiful" is a highly complex phenomenon including elements that shade off into and are also contained in other sorts of experiences.

For example: "Sublime" is both an aesthetic and religious category. According to The Shorter Oxford English Dictionary (3rd edition), when applied to things in nature and art the term means "calculated to inspire awe, deep reverence, or lofty emotion, by reason of beauty, vastness, or grandeur." When I listen to Handel's Messiah I experience sublimity in precisely that sense. The "awe, deep reverence, ..[and] lofty emotion" I feel also modify my existence at least momentarily: my being is elevated, ennobled, "sublimated" (in Nietzsche's sense of the "subliming" or spiritualizing of our basic needs and drives), healed. These are all qualities of religious experience, and--to use a starkly contrasting example to illustrate the point--one can also enjoy them in the silence of a Quaker meeting.

But the point is that to experience sublimity hearing Handel's Messiah is to experience it under the aspect of artistic beauty. Experience of the Messiah is a Gestalt in which I am simultaneously aware of the aesthetic elements producing sublimity: the marvellously felicitous wedding of music and biblical text; the interesting variation and combination of orchestral, choral, and solo parts; the quality of musical themes and harmonies. Obviously, at least in my own case, the familiar texts from the Hebrew Bible and the New Testament are an ingredient in the "religiousness" of my experience of the Messiah. But there are other works that I regard as sublime that have nothing to do with biblical material, such as the choral movement of Beethoven's Ninth Symphony, some of

Purcell's and Vivaldi's trumpet music, and Moussorgsky-Ravel's "Great Gate of Kiev" from Pictures at an Exhibition. To ask the question, Where does the "aesthetic" leave off and the "religious" begin?, is to misunderstand the experience of sublimity through beauty. It is precisely the beauty of the Messiah that is the vehicle of my experience of it as gracious.

The same case could be made for our common experience of the moral as an element in the experience of beauty. Dickens and Tolstoy, Camus and Wiesel are novelists of moral profundity and passion. They challenge and inspire us with moral questioning, vision, courage, and compassion. But they do it in a uniquely powerful artistic way rather than by writing ethical treatises. Where does the aesthetic end and the moral begin in their fiction? To read their novels is to realize that the question is not rightly put. The moral dimension is an important and integral element in their beauty and cannot be neatly abstracted from it without serious distortion. In both the Messiah and the works of the novelists I have mentioned we would want to say that we experience them as gracious precisely by experiencing them as beautiful. There would be something both odd and dismal in saying that one listens to the Messiah in order to "get religion out of it" or reads Anna Karenina in order to "draw moral lessons" from it. It is rather that in experiencing them as works of richly complex beauty we experience in them the holy and the ethical but quite rightly want to label the whole as "beautiful."

To recur to the point from which I began this essay: the experience of beauty as grace is not only one of the most important of the many things that lighten our darkness; for some persons without religious faith beauty bears some of the marks of divinity and its experience the quality of faith. There is a mystery, an otherness, a timelessness about many of the expressions of both human and natural beauty when they are received as grace. And the receiving itself is an ecstasy, a self-transcending resonant with feeling, through which the human spirit is granted vision and restoration, wholeness and reunion, if only for a moment at a time. The manifestations of earthly beauty and the experience of their graciousness can function as powerfully and "savingly" in the lives of agnostics and atheists as God and faith in the lives of religious believers, an example of which we saw in considering Camus's "victory over the world" in Chapter One.

Our experiences of the graciousness of beauty, like all our experiences of the good, are fragmentary and fragile. But human life deprived of them becomes intolerable. Viktor Frankl recounts that in the Nazi concentration camps, which represent one of the most thorough attempts in history systematically to strip human beings of all the things that make us think of ourselves as human, those prisoners who managed to preserve something of their inner life "experienced the beauty of art and nature as never before."[6] Frankl provides a few moving examples, of which the following can serve as illustration:

> One evening, when we were already resting on the floor of our hut, dead tired, soup bowls in hand, a fellow prisoner rushed in and asked us to run out to the assembly grounds and see the wonderful sunset. Standing outside we saw sinister clouds glowing in the west and the whole sky alive with clouds of ever-changing shapes and colors, from steel blue to blood red. The desolate gray mud huts provided a sharp contrast, while the puddles on the muddy ground reflected the glowing sky. Then, after minutes of moving silence, one prisoner said to another, "How beautiful the world could be!"[7]

Frankl also speaks of attempts at art of various sorts amid those unspeakable conditons. For those who were still able to receive it, what small measure of earth's beauties was available was sheer grace: one of their pitifully few sources of meaning, strength, consolation, and self-transcendence. Most human beings long for any hint of beauty amid whatever desolation and drabness is their lot without or within, unless they have been totally crushed by circumstances. And they long for it because of its grace, because it is living water to parched tongues and mud-caked bodies. That water may have its origins beyond the world, or it may not; whatever its source, it is baptism and eucharist to all who experience it.

FOOTNOTES

[1] Anders Nygren, _Agape and Eros_, trans. by Philip S. Watson, Philadelphia: The Westminster Press, 1953, p. 91.

[2] The theme runs throughout my book _Borderland Christianity: Critical Reason and the Christian Vision of Love_ (Nashville: Abingdon, 1973), but is treated specifically in Ch. VIII.

[3] In this connection I continue to be intrigued by the theory of religion as a form of moral perspective advanced by R. B. Braithwaite in his much-discussed lecture "An Empiricist's View of the Nature of Religious Belief," in John Hick, ed., _The Existence of God_, N.Y.: Macmillan, 1964, pp. 228-252. While obviously unsatisfactory as a theory of religion, it contains interesting insights about the relationship between religion and ethics.

[4] N. Richard Nash, _The Rainmaker_, N.Y.: Bantam, 1957, p. 99; quoted in Joseph Fletcher, _Situation Ethics_, Philadelphia: Westminster Press, 1966, p. 13.

[5] See, e.g., his _Systematic Theology_, Vol. I, Chicago: University of Chicago Press, 1951, pp. 12-14.

[6] _Man's Search for Meaning_, N.Y.: Washington Square Press, 1963, p. 62.

[7] Pp. 62-63.

111

EPILOGUE

CHARLIE CITRINE AND THE ARGUMENT FROM ABSURDITY

I suspect that some readers of this essay wonder who in the world Charlie Citrine is. Let me begin here at the very outset to relieve your suspense: Charlie Citrine is the protagonist of Saul Bellow's extraordinary novel Humboldt's Gift.[1] I want to add to that revelation another prefatory remark, this one a disclaimer: I'm not a Saul Bellow expert. This is not a literary-critical study of Bellow but a philosophical presentation of the ideas of one of his characters; something along the lines of Robert Champigny's book A Pagan Hero, which was not a study of Camus or even of The Stranger but rather of its protagonist Meursault.[2] At the same time, Charlie Citrine's thinking is all the more intriguing when we realize that in him Bellow has created a character who is more than a little autobiographical.

What I propose to do is to examine Charlie Citrine as a powerful and haunting contemporary literary expression of an old and many-faceted case for supernaturalism: what I call the "argument from absurdity." I'm using "absurdity" in the somewhat technical sense that Camus gave it. He used the term to describe the incommensurability between what he called our "nostalgia" for ultimate meaning, clarity and fulfillment on the one hand, and the circumstances of our existence as earthly creatures dependent upon our physical nature and environment on the other. Camus believed that religions and many philosophies are forms of "faith" that try in various ways to overcome this incommensurability by leaping over the "absurd walls" of our condition and interpreting human beings and the world in terms of an ultimate reality and transcendent meaning undergirding it all. As is well known, Camus himself rejected all such forms of faith and attempted, in his words, to "live only with what I know"--to remain within the context of the absurd situation "without appeal" beyond it.[3]

But of course for centuries religious thinkers and many philosophers have taken this very incommensurability between human desires and the human situation precisely as evidence for the reality of a transcendent order of being of which the visible world and our empirical egos are only a finite manifestation or creation. The myriad ways in which our human reach exceeds our grasp--which on this reasoning are indeed absurd and pathetic if we are no more than brief products of evolutionary "chance and necessity"--are so many intimations of who we really are, what reality is really like, and what our true destiny really is. This argument is a form of the traditional appeal to the principle of sufficient reason: If beings appear in the world with capacities, wants, imaginings, and aspirations that the world cannot completely fulfill, any explanation that is fully adequate to the phenomenon must be one that can sufficiently ground them and assure their fulfillment. Such an explanation, the reasoning goes, requires that reality be more than the world and that we ourselves be more than this frail physical creature who "struts and frets his hour upon the stage / And then is heard no more."[4]

In the Christian tradition this argumentum de absurdo finds its epigram in Augustine's famous address to God in the Confessions: "Thou hast made us for Thyself, and our hearts are restless till they find their rest in Thee." The argument achieves its most acute, explicit, and sustained expression in the writings of Søren Kierkegaard. Kierkegaard's whole authorship can be seen as a series of brilliantly original and perceptive variations on the one theme that in its essence the self is what he calls "spirit" or "eternal consciousness" created by and destined ultimately for fellowship with God. Two central, closely related expressions of this theme in his writings are of particular significance for my study of Charlie Citrine, whose ideas are in some important respects strikingly Kierkegaardian. The first is the famous either/or, the ultimate and finally unrationalizable choice that confronts every human being in every present: either the many varieties of the conventional knowledge and worldliness, through which I never come to self-knowledge; or the daring venture of inwardness that discovers to me my

"eternal validity" and finds its ownmost end in the
leap of faith through which I acknowledge in thought
and deed my own spirit's ground and destiny in the
Eternal Spirit. And as Judge William points out in
Either/or, "The choice itself is decisive for the
content of the personality, through the choice the
personality immerses itself in the thing chosen . .
. "[5]

The second and corollary idea is despair.
Kierkegaard's book The Sickness Unto Death is of
course a sustained exploration of the secret and
overt forms of despair that he believed characterize
all selves insofar as we live our lives unwilling to
dare that final leap of trust in our eternal
grounding in the Eternal. Most of us live our lives
in hidden despair, more or less unconsciously
dispersed in the demands and distractions of the
all-too-thickly-real world around us. Some of us
bring our despair to conscious focus, thereby
succeeding in making ourselves explicitly miserable.
Such conscious despair is a necessary dialectical
moment in the development of the self; but typically
we stick fast in it and never get beyond melancholy
introversion or proud defiance. Anti-Climacus, the
author of The Sickness Unto Death, grieves over the
despairing condition of humankind in a passage that
would have moved Charlie Citrine deeply:

> . . . only that man's life is wasted who
> lived on, so deceived by the joys of life or
> by its sorrows that he never became
> eternally and decisively conscious of
> himself as spirit, as self, or (what is the
> same thing) never became aware and in the
> deepest sense received an impression of the
> fact that there is a God. . . . And, oh,
> this misery, that so many live on and are
> defrauded of this most blessed of all
> thoughts; this misery, that people employ
> themselves about everything else. . . . --it
> seems to me that I could weep for an
> eternity over the fact that such misery
> exists![6]

If persons are indeed finite creatures designed
for an eternal relationship or union with the
Infinite, we should not be surprised that this

finite theatre in which we act out our lives is not made to our measure. Probably the chief contribution of "depth" theologians like Augustine and Kierkegaard lies in having profoundly explored the many ramifications of this "absurd" situation: our restless desires for meaning and fulfillment, goodness and knowledge, union and ecstasy, which manifest themselves in such exquisite and such grotesque ways; the intolerable acuteness of our bondage and suffering seen in the light of our hunger for ultimate significance and perdurance. These are just what we would expect if it turns out to be the case that we are indeed finite beings for whom the finite is not finally our "home."

Enter Charlie Citrine: well-known American biographer and playwright, twice Pulitzer Prize winner. Now pushing sixty, Charlie was born of Russian immigrant parents in Appleton, Wisconsin-- also the birthplace of Harry Houdini, with whom he feels a metaphysical kinship because of their common preoccupation with the problem of death--but grew up in the Polish section of Chicago and has returned in recent years to Chicago to live.

Charlie finds himself painfully "waking up" from what he feels has been a lifetime of spiritual sleepwalking. His life crisis has been brought about by reflections on the death several years before of his old friend Von Humboldt Fleisher, a poet who after brilliant early promise and success with his Harlequin Ballads went to seed, flipped out, ended up on Skid Row, and died in Bellevue. An awesomely well-read American literary intellectual (like Bellow himself), Charlie is blessed/cursed with what Dostoevsky's Underground Man called hyperconsciousness. He reflects endlessly on the persons and events around him in terms of the Big Questions. But through Humboldt's death Charlie becomes completely absorbed in the Big Question of death, which, he reminds us, "Walt Whitman saw as the question of questions." (63) Charlie begins to meditate almost obsessively not only upon his friend Humboldt, but also upon his other beloved dead: his parents, and a former lover named Demmie Vonghel who was killed in a plane crash. He feels a deep loyalty to his dead and a sense of responsibility towards them for what he does with the rest of his own life.

Death, then, is the overriding issue for Charlie, the touchstone of his awakening. Preoccupation with death is an expression of Charlie's temperament that is closely connected with other temperamental factors which are the personal ground of his version of the "argument from absurdity." To recognize these emotional roots is for me decidedly not a reductionistic exercise, since it is entirely possible that some persons are dispositionally more receptive to various sorts of truths--if truths they be. I begin with these personal factors because they illuminate the existential eros propelling Charlie's quest for meaning, and provide an important paradigm of some central features of the human situation to which the argumentum de absurdo appeals. By his own admission, Charlie is temperamentally melancholic, sentimental, and nostalgic. His melancholy reminds us a bit of Kierkegaard: there is an undertone of yearning sadness and depression as Charlie contemplates his own self-contradictory existence and the comically-tragically despairing lives of the human beings around him. He is furthermore shamelessly sentimental, often inwardly overcome by deep-seated feelings of love towards persons from his past and his present. But it is Charlie's nostalgia that gathers up the other temperamental factors into an existential foundation for his "argument from absurdity," and unites them with his preoccupation with death. Charlie acutely embodies that universal aspect of human sensibility characterized by the German word Sehnsucht, which literally means "longing" or "yearning." In his study of C. S. Lewis, Bright Shadow of Reality, Corbin Scott Carnell depicts Sehnsucht in this way: "The crucial concept in defining this attitude is best expressed in English by the word 'nostalgia.' Even though Sehnsucht may be made up of several components or appear in different forms (melancholy, wonder, yearning, etc.), basic to its various manifestations is an underlying sense of displacement or alienation from what is desired." Elsewhere he describes it similarly as "a sense of separation from what is desired, a ceaseless longing which always points beyond." All this profoundly and essentially describes Charlie Citrine, who himself characterizes "my lifelong trouble--the longing, the swelling heart, the tearing eagerness of the deserted, the painful keenness or infinitizing of an unidentified need." (401) I think we can readily see how his sentimentality, his melancholy, and his preoccupation with death are all integral elements in his nostalgia. I trust that it is also clear how this <u>Sehnsucht</u>, this "ceaseless longing which always points beyond," provides the dispositional basis for the "argument from absurdidty."

I want in the remainder of my essay to look at four elements in Charlie Citrine's version of the absurdict argument: (1) its conceptual focus on immortality and its philosophical framework in Platonic idealism; (2) Charlie's disillusionment with the dominant scientific positivism, with "rational orthodoxy" as he calls it (351), and his plea on behalf of the intuitive, poetic imagination as true knowledge of being; (3) the despair in which humans in the modern world live, a despair that manifests itself in an all-pervasive boredom and sloth; and (4) the either/or, the choice: <u>either</u> the prevailing, ultimately despairing view of life and death that pervades our collective consciousness; <u>or</u> the affirmation of our immortality and the "great chain of being" which is the soul's true context.

1. Since the "death question" is the Big Question for Charlie, it's not surprising that the chief emphasis in his fitful spiritual awakening from what he calls his "deep snooze" (295) is the transcendent nature of the self; specifically, its immortality. A central theme in Charlie's new perspective on reality is the Platonic one-- expressed philosophically in the <u>Meno</u> and the <u>Phaedo</u> and poetically in Wordsworth's "Ode: Intimations of Immortality"--that we are eternally existing souls whose birth in the temporal world is "a sleep and a forgetting" of who we really are. Sleep is the key image Charlie uses to describe his own spiritual condition for most of his life, and he considers what he calls the "will-to-snooze" (283) endemic to the alienation from our true identity and ground that characterizes human beings generally.[9] Like

117

Wordsworth, Charlie believes that young children briefly retain, through wonder and imagination, a sense of who they really are, but that this is soon stifled by the conventional knowledge and practice of adult society. Yet some persons, like Charlie himself, are temperamentally disposed to be consciously haunted and taunted by that inchoate, largely repressed sense of our spiritual nature and immortality which characterizes human beings generally. "I had never doubted that I had such a thing [as an immortal spirit]," Charlie observes. "But I had set this fact aside quite early. I kept it under my hat." (105) We see in this dominant Citrinean motif one clear and classic expression of Sehnsucht: a sense of separation from and longing for one's essential nature and ground, one's primal union with being.

Perhaps not surprisingly, the conceptual form that Charlie's reflections on immortality take is a broadly Platonic philosophical idealism. Early on in the book he characterizes his friend Humboldt's Harlequin Ballads as "Platonic," and explains that the term refers to "an original perfection to which all human beings long to return." (10) Charlie espouses such explicitly Platonic ideas as pre-existence and reincarnation. Several times throughout the book he appeals specifically to Plato, as in the following passage:

What a human being is--I always had my own odd sense of this . . . . I was drawn. . . to philosophical idealists because I was perfectly sure that this could not be it. Plato in the Myth of Er confirmed my sense that this was not my first time around. We had all been here before and would presently be here again. There was another place. (86)

But the specific form of philosophical idealism in which Charlie becomes thoroughly immersed and through which his spiritual awakening takes place is the anthroposophy of Rudolf Steiner. Steiner's work is closely related to the late nineteenth- and early twentieth-century theosophical movement, but he attained lasting respectability because his speculations were believed by many to be more

118

solidly grounded in scientific knowledge and more rational and systematic than were those of the theosophists. At the same time, one finds in his writings the wildly imaginative flights, the esoteric religious eclecticism, and the endless hierarchical schema of the soul and the world that characterize theosophical literature generally. One thing that attracts Charlie to Steiner is precisely these free flights of metaphysical and religious imagination in contrast to the prosaic, relentlessly earth-bound inquiries and conclusions of "rational orthodoxy."

But despite its large material role in the novel--which I think is to be accounted for by Bellow's own serious involvement in anthroposophy-- my own view is that formally speaking Steiner's philosophy is simply a vehicle or medium of a much more general metaphysical choice which Charlie is making and with which he confronts us. It is not even Charlie's Platonism generally, his specific beliefs in pre-existence and reincarnation, that are at the heart of the matter. What is essential to the novel's "message" is rather Charlie's being gripped by one articulation of what Huston Smith calls the "primordial tradition":[10] a universal vision of human beings as grounded in and destined for the Eternal, and of reality as more than the visible world; a vision that expresses itself in many particular forms. What is at issue is Charlie's absorbing conviction that we are confronted by an either/or, by fundamental choices between alternative interpretations of what is real; and that the type of interpretation he is in the process of choosing belongs to the only class of world-views that finally renders our crazy lives and cold deaths coherent and meaningful. Plato expressed it through Orphic myths; Augustine and Kierkegaard through Christian myths; and Steiner through theosophical myths.

At one point Charlie alludes to what he calls "esthetic grounds" for his belief in immortality: "On esthetic grounds, if on no others, I cannot accept the view of death taken by most of us, and taken by me during most of my life--on esthetic grounds therefore I am obliged to deny that so extraordinary a thing as a human soul can be wiped out forever." (136) Charlie's "esthetic grounds" are an appeal to the intuitively creative realm of human imagination whose priests and prophets are the poets. This appeal brings me to the second element in his "argument from absurdity."

2. Now that some measure of light has been graciously vouchsafed him, Charlie Citrine has become thoroughly disillusioned with the reigning scientific models of knowledge, truth, and relation to reality. He issues a passionate plea for the recovery of what he calls the "imaginative soul," our profounder self more profoundly in touch with ourselves and reality. Charlie comes to realize that this was his friend Humboldt's poetic legacy: "The imagination must not pine away--that was Humboldt's message. It must assert again that art manifests the inner powers of nature." (107-108) Humboldt, Charlie believes, was finally crushed, vise-like, between a rationalistic orthodoxy which considers poetic imagination an epiphenomenal madness, on the one hand, and on the other its pragmatic bedfellow a gross American materialism that subordinates all other values to those of production and consumption.

Charlie is convinced that "there is far more to any experience, connection, or relationship than ordinary consciousness, the daily life of the ego, can grasp." (321) He pursues this notion also when he remarks on his understanding of what religion is:

What does religion say? It says that there's something in human beings beyond the body and brain and that we have ways of knowing that go beyond the organism and its senses. I've always believed that. My misery comes, maybe, from ignoring my own metaphysical hunches. I've been to college so I know the educated answers. Test me on the scientific world-view and I'd score high. But it's just head stuff. (219)

Charlie pleads for the multidimensionality of both knowledge and reality, for the validity of those personal, intuitive, and imaginative connections that ordinary people have with being:

It comes to this, that the individual has no way to prove out what's in his heart--I mean the love, the hungering for the external world, the swelling excitement over beauty for which there are no acceptable terms of knowledge. True knowledge is supposed to be a monopoly of the scientific world view. But human beings have all sorts of knowledge. They don't have to apply for the right to love the world. (352)

This conviction of the ontological authenticity of our concrete imaginative relations with the world finds its most carefully articulated expression in Charlie's discussions of disenchantment. I find these discussions especially evocative of just the sort of thing that thinkers like Heidegger, Marcel, and Buber have sought to get at in a more formal way with their varied attempts to illuminate, and evoke assent to, the integrity of existential modes of knowledge and being over against the ruling "calculative" models. In a running commentary on a major essay he wants to write on boredom--a commentary that is a brilliant Bellovian tour de force--Charlie provocatively criticizes the scientific world-view for disenchanting the world:

. . . our world-view has used up nature. The rule of this view is that I, a subject, see the phenomena, the world of objects. They, however, are not necessarily in themselves objects as modern rationality defines objects. For in spirit, says Steiner, a man can step out of himself and let things speak to him about themselves, to speak about what has meaning not for him alone but also for them. Thus the sun the moon the stars will speak to non-astronomers in spite of their ignorance of science. In fact it's high time that this happened. Ignorance of science should not keep one imprisoned in the lowest and weariest sector of being, prohibited from entering into independent relations with the creation as a whole. The educated speak of the disenchanted (a boring) world. But it is not the world, it is my own head that is

121

disenchanted. The world <u>cannot</u> be
<u>disenchanted</u>. (195; first italics mine)

In a later discussion of disenchantment, Charlie
similarly insists that the problem is that "our
minds. . . have allowed themselves to be convinced
that there is no imaginative power to connect every
individual to the creation independently." (352)

It is the poet (actually the artist generally,
but for obvious reasons Charlie singles out the
poet) who brings the true view, the "enchanted"
view, of being to supreme and normative expression.
Charlie asks rhetorically, "why should poetry refuse
to be knowledge?" (351) The poet, through his or
her creative development and articulation of the
"imaginative soul" that slumbers in every human
being, is par excellence a "seer": a person with
concrete insight, to use Tillich's phrase, into
"dimensions and elements of reality which otherwise
would remain unapproachable. . . [and] elements of
our soul which correspond to the dimensions and
elements of reality."[11]

3. "The world's distraction, activity, [and]
noise" manifest and reinforce our forgetfulness of
being--of our own reality and the depths of reality
in which it is grounded. For Charlie Citrine, as
for Kierkegaard, this forgetfulness of being is
finally despair. Charlie examines despair under two
closely related headings: boredom and sloth. Not
surprisingly, both have a certain relationship to
sleep or lack of consciousness.

I've mentioned that Charlie is working on a
major study of boredom: a kind of phenomenology and
history of boredom. He considers Kierkegaard, by
the way, one of the great experts on boredom (104),
and intends to examine his contribution in his own
essay (195). Charlie considers boredom the serious
malaise especially of the modern technologized
world. He calls boredom a "deep suffering," (104)
and the hypothesis of his essay is that boredom is
"a kind of pain caused by unused power, the pain of
wasted possibilities or talents." (192) Clearly at
the profoundest level boredom thus defined is the
metaphysical suffering brought about by our
forgetting our ownmost self, our immortal

imaginative soul that establishes our true connection with being, and dispersing ourselves in an environment of endless distraction, mindless activity, and numbing noise. It is an environment that furthermore proclaims in both its praxis and its knowledge that THIS IS IT and THIS IS ALL.

Sloth is the other category under which Charlie considers despair. The common view that sloth is simple laziness, he says, is wrong; sloth is actually a relentless busy-ness, precisely because "sloth has to cover a great deal of despair."

Sloth is really a busy condition, hyperactive. This activity drives off the wonderful rest or balance without which there can be no poetry or art or thought-- none of the highest human functions. These slothful sinners are not able to acquiesce in their own being, as some philosophers say. They labor because rest terrifies them. The old philosophy distinguished between knowledge achieved by effort (ratio) and knowledge received (intellectus) by the listening soul that can hear the essence of things and comes to understand the marvelous. But this calls for strength of soul. The more so since society claims more and more of your inner self and infects you with its restlessness. It trains you in distraction, colonizes consciousness as fast as consciousness advances. (295)

Sloth, then, is a phenomenal hyperactivity cloaking a metaphysical torpor, an inner lack of "strength of soul" which is despair. Charlie goes on to confess that he has been the chief of "slothful sinners" until the very recent awakening that has only just begun, haltingly and fitfully, to bring a little order and light into his own crazy existence. Boredom, then, is the pain of the soul's powers slumbering untapped amid a world of empty distractions; sloth is the restless activity that masks the soul's stupefied inability to rest in its own being and ground: what are these but forms of that inauthentic sleep that is our despairing condition?

4. Again like Kierkegaard, Charlie believes that he and all of us are confronted by basic choices about the whole way we are to comprehend and live out our lives: choices _from_ which all sorts of implications flow in life and knowledge, but _for_ which reasons are never sufficient. For Charlie it is _either_ the dominant positivism and hedonism which spell despair, _or_ being faithful to those intuitive-imaginative intimations that we and the reality that embraces us possess wondrous depths of which we are hardly aware. Charlie is quite clear about the fateful demand to come to a decision about this issue. He spells out the choice, of course, primarily in terms of the "death question," and presents it first in relation to his personal loyalty to his beloved dead. Reflecting on his sessions with his anthroposophy teacher, Dr. Scheldt, he puts the matter starkly:

. . . there were the dead to think of. Unless I had utterly lost interest in them, unless I were satisfied to feel only a secular melancholy about my mother and father or Demmie Vonghel or Von Humboldt Fleisher, I was obliged to investigate, to satisfy myself that death _was_ final, that the dead _were_ dead. _Either_ I conceded the finality of death and refused to have any further intimations, condemned my childish sentimentality and hankering, _or_ I conducted a full and proper investigation. Because I simply didn't see how I could refuse to investigate. Yes, I could force myself to think of it all as the irretrievable loss of shipmates to the devouring Cyclops. I could think of the human scene as a battlefield. The fallen are put into holes in the ground or burned to ash. After this, you are not supposed to inquire after the man who gave you life, the woman who bore you, after a Demmie whom you had last seen getting into a plane at Idlewild with her big blond legs and her make-up and her earrings, or after the brilliant golden master of conversation Von Humboldt Fleisher, whom you had last beheld eating a pretzel in the West Forties. You could simply assume that they had been forever wiped out, as you too would one day be. So if the daily papers told of murders committed in the streets before crowds of neutral witnesses, there was nothing illogical about such neutrality. On the metaphysical assumptions about death everyone in the world had apparently reached, everyone would be snatched, ravished by death, throttled, smothered. This terror and this murdering were the most natural things in the world. And these same conclusions were incorporated into the life of society and present in all its institutions, in politics, education, banking, justice. Convinced of this, I saw no reason why I shouldn't go to Dr. Scheldt to talk about Seraphim and Cherubim and Thrones and Dominions and Exousiai and Archai and Angels and Spirits. (254, italicizing of *Either* and *or* mine)

I want to call attention here to Charlie's notion that, absurdity for absurdity--"dupery for dupery," as Will James charcteristically put it in a somewhat different context--on what possible grounds is it crazier to entertain the possibility that the visionary speculations of a Rudolf Steiner are true than to accept the brutally grotesque picture of humankind enshrined in the prevailing *Zeitgeist* and its institutions?

Later Charlie describes his involvement with anthroposophy as a kind of "leap of faith":

I meant to make a strange jump and plunge into the truth. I had had it with most contemporary ways of philosophizing. Once and for all I was going to find out whether there was anything behind the incessant hints of immortality that kept dropping on me. (344-345)

Throughout *Humboldt's Gift* Charlie considers his commitment to Steiner's philosophy to be one that embraces the skeptical doubts he brings to it from his lifetime of education and habituation in the reality-picture of "rational orthodoxy." But he is willing to plunge into the new perspective, to take its view and its ethics absolutely seriously and

adopt its approach to meditation, because it rings
essentially true in the light of those many
manifestations of Sehnsucht that he finds in himself
and in human life generally.

Charlie even states his case for making the
decisive choice in the form of a "wager" argument:

> Suppose, then, that after the greatest,
> most passionate vividness and tender glory,
> oblivion is all we have to expect, the big
> blank of death. What options present
> themselves? One option is to train yourself
> gradually into oblivion so that no great
> change has taken place when you have died.
> Another option is to increase the bitterness
> of life so that death is a desirable
> release. (In this the rest of mankind will
> fully collaborate.) There is a further
> option seldom chosen. That option is to let
> the deepest elements in you disclose their
> deepest information. If there is nothing
> but nonbeing and oblivion waiting for us,
> the prevailing beliefs have not misled us,
> and that's that. This would astonish me,
> for the prevailing beliefs seldom satisfy my
> need for truth. Still the possibility must
> be allowed. Suppose, however, that oblivion
> is not the case? What, then, have I been
> doing for about six decades? I think that I
> never believed that oblivion was the case
> and by five and a half decades of distortion
> and absurdity I have challenged and disputed
> the alleged rationality and finality of the
> oblivion view. (345)

Some of Charlie's above remarks are a bit
reminiscent of Unamuno's own passionate choice of
immortality when he wrote that "we must feel and act
as if an endless continuation of our earthly life
awaited us after death; and if it be that
nothingness is the fate that awaits us we must not.
. . so act that it shall be a just fate."[12]

Again, Charlie characterizes his choice as a
"postulate," in a passage in which he expresses both
his disdain for the prevailing models of knowledge
and reality and his confessed ambivalence, as a

deep-dyed product of those models, about aspects of Steiner's thought:

> My postulate was that there was a core of the eternal in every human being. Had this been a mental or logical problem I would have dealt logically with it. However, it was no such thing. What I had to deal with was a lifelong intimation. This intimation must be either a tenacious illusion or else the truth deeply buried. The mental respectability of good members of educated society was something I had come to despise with all my heart. I admit that I was sustained by contempt whenever. . . [Steiner's] esoteric texts made me uneasy. For there were passages in Steiner that set my teeth on edge. I said to myself, this is lunacy. Then I said, this is poetry, a great vision. But I went on with it. . . . The strangeness of life: the more you resisted it, the harder it bore down on you. The more the mind opposed the sense of strangeness, the more distortions it produced. (424; my italics)

Charlie's remarks on the "strangeness" of life, of reality, and the distortions produced by "rational orthodoxy" in opposing that fact, importantly recall that ceaseless wonder over the "queerness of things" that was at the heart of both Kierkegaard's and C. S. Lewis's reflections.

What I have been calling the "argument from absurdity" and exploring in a sort of cumulative way in the thought of Charlie Citrine finds explicit expression in his statement that "I was convinced that there was nothing in the material world to account for the more delicate desires and perceptions of human beings. . . There was no basis in common experience," he goes on to say,

> for the Good, the True, and the Beautiful. And I was too queerly haughty to take stock in the respectable empiricism in which I had been educated. Too many fools subscribed to it. Besides, people were not really surprised when you spoke to them about the

soul and the spirit. How odd! No one was
surprised. Sophisticated people were the
only ones who expressed surprise. (425)

Charlie later returns to this theme, and relates it
to our common despair and the boredom that is one of
its manifestations:

We feel suffocated and don't know why.
The existence of a soul is beyond proof
under the ruling premises, but people go on
behaving as though they had souls
nevertheless. They behave as if they came
from another place, another life, and they
have impulses and desires that nothing in
this world, none of our present premises,
can account for. On the ruling premises the
fate of humankind is a sporting event, most
ingenious. Fascinating. When it doesn't
become boring. The specter of boredom is
haunting this sporting conception of
history. (463)

As I've pointed out more than once, and as
Charlie Citrine's own statements abundantly
indicate, his chief preoccupation is the nature of
the soul and its transcending of death. But as
we've also seen, especially in the section on the
imaginative soul and its authentic relationship to
being, Charlie doesn't omit that to which the
imaginative soul responds in its perceivings:
reality that is more than the sensible world;
reality as eternal and richly multidimensional being
of which the visible world and our earthly lives are
only one sort of manifestation. As part of his
choosing against the reigning skepticism, Charlie
reaffirms that aesthetically sublime, hierarchical
vision of the cosmos which the ancient world and
classical Christianity espoused as virtually self-
evident: what Lovejoy called the "great chain of
being" from the most rudimentary forms of inorganic
matter through vegetable, animal, and human life
through hierarchies of angels to God. At one point
Charlie describes his awakening in this way: "I
seemed to be recovering an independent and
individual connection with the creation, the whole
hierarchy of being." (427) Elsewhere he contrasts
what we too glibly absolutize as the "human scale"

with a "different scale": "The question is this: why should we assume that the series ends with us? The fact is, I suspect, that we occupy a point within a great hierarchy that goes far far beyond ourselves." (463)

Saul Bellow is of course a consummate portrayer of the complicated craziness and endless self-contradictions of the human tragicomedy, always doing so with both hilarity and deep compassion. The theme of absurdity in Humboldt's Gift is only intensified and reinforced by the "absurdities"--in the more everyday sense of the word--of Charlie Citrine's life. The reader is treated to the sometimes ludicrous, sometimes painful juxtaposition of his anthroposophical "higher" meditations and his all-too-earthbound, frantically jumbled situation. His wife Denise is in the process of divorcing him and "taking" him for everything he is worth. His voluptuously beautiful lover Renata (the most recent in what Charlie calls his "woman-filled life" [107]) measures everything by its erotic significance and in her simplicity wants Charlie to marry her. He is pursued by a Chicago Mafia-type mobster, Rinaldo Cantabile, one of those "men of the world" to whom Charlie, a comparatively innocent "ivory tower" intellectual, is secretly drawn. Charlie continues to indulge his extravagantly expensive tastes in clothes, travel, and food while he is rapidly going broke. And just as we have fully realized that Humboldt's posthumous "gift" to Charlie is really the latter's spiritual awakening, it turns out that the more tangible legacy he bequeaths to him in the form of two movie scenarios ends up netting Charlie about $100,000 and solving his acute financial problems. Happily, by this time Charlie has finally turned his back on all that and begun living simply, uses the money largely to help other persons, and is ready to head off to the Steiner Center in Dornach, Switzerland. The sense of mission, of responsibility to his beloved dead and to the world, that has grown steadily since his awakening, has now thoroughly gripped him:

Actuarially speaking, I had only a decade left to make up for a life-span largely misspent. There was no time to waste even on remorse and penitence. I felt

also that Humboldt, out there in death,
stood in need of my help. The dead and the
living still formed one community. . . .
There was Humboldt's bungled life, and my
bungled life, and it was up to me to do
something, to give a last favorable turn to
the wheel, to transmit moral understanding
from the earth where you can get it to the
next existence where you needed it. (392)

For me the "absurdities" of Charlie Citrine's
life only reinforce existentially his presentation
of the "argument from absurdity," because they are
so warmly and poignantly paradigmatic of all the
ways in which most of us with the best of intentions
stumble through life's situations and relationships.
Bound up closely with this is my very personal
identification with Charlie's dominant feelings, his
endless reflections, and his impassioned spiritual
quest--all jostling with one another and with life's
all-too-earthbound demands and dailyness.

To conclude: I confess that I find what I have
called the "argument from absurdity" probably the
most compelling among the various sorts of cases
that have been made for transcendental
interpretations of ourselves and the world. I have
presented Saul Bellow's character Charlie Citrine's
views as a recent literary expression of this old
argument that I find particularly arresting and
eloquent. While I by no means accept the Platonic
and anthroposophical framework which is the
particular intellectual vehicle of Charlie's own
reflections, I have also suggested that this should
be seen as simply his peculiar variation of a
general alternative which articulates itself in many
ways. I am especially stimulated, as one who has
spent his adult life torn between a skeptical
rationalism and the claims of religious traditions,
by Charlie's reflections on the validity of our
concrete, intuitive-imaginative relations with the
world. Of course I have been reading all this sort
of thing for years in the writings of people like
Kierkegaard, Buber, Marcel, and Heidegger; but
somehow it has come freshly alive once again through
reading Humboldt's Gift. And for me at least this
epistemological hurdle is the absolutely crucial one
to clear in order to open up the ontological

integrity of the realms of existential relationship and imagination such as art and religion. It is not at all insignificant to me, of course, that it is precisely a work of the imagination--a novel--that has vividly and provocatively reopened my thinking about the issue.

Clearly, to say that arguments for the transcendence of human being and being itself on the basis of the absurdity or incommensurability of our situation considered otherwise are powerful and arresting, is by no means to say that they are demonstrative. To the _argumentum de absurdo_ in its many forms there is alway the entirely reasonable and correct skeptical response that the peculiarities of the human species do not in any way logically entail a transcendent explanation. The principle of sufficient reason remains for some thinkers the compelling demand inherent in the very nature and dynamic of reason; but for most it has become a problematic, undemonstrable, and unnecessary assumption. We may genuinely be a "useless passion," a crazy product of the evolutionary process, and these transcending desires and seeming glimpses simply wishes that fly in the face of reality--in Freud's terms _illusions_ that are almost certainly also _delusionary_. The naturalistic humanist, from ancient times to the present, characteristically urges that this physical globe is our proper and only context as physical creatures of the earth; that we shall find real happiness and fulfillment only by accepting the fact and tailoring our desires to reality so defined.

Then there are the more specific sorts of problems which I have raised in earlier essays of this book. I simply cannot reconcile certain important symbols of transcendence with the world as we know it, filled as it is with so much gratuitous human suffering. To this I must add my philosophical difficulties with the very notions of the soul and immortality. The whole thrust of my discussions in previous essays of our creaturely dependence and our psychological bondage was a soberly earth-bound, ineradicably psychophysical characterization of human existence. These problems are real, the data to which I have appealed are

formidable, and the purely secular conclusions I
have drawn seem to me to be persuasive.

And yet. . . . I admitted even in my despairing
Prologue that I remained quite open to all sorts of
transcendent possibilities. I cannot render them
coherent any more at the end of this book than I
could at the beginning; I must still content myself
with the earthly that I know and assume that if
there is more to reality it may some day reveal
itself to me. The only "divinity" that I experience
is the Christly immanence of what seem to be the
purely human and natural graces of truth, beauty,
and goodness. But I continue to be nagged, uneasy,
divided: Precisely that glaring incongruity between
the world I know and the vision of transcendence
seems at times a prophetic voice crying in the
wilderness rather than simply an anguished cry in
the night. Absurdity indeed has two faces; it is a
Janus bifrons--and I, schizophrenically, am two
personae in response to it.

And like Charlie Citrine, I feel perpetually
split between the rational-empirical and the
imaginative-intuitive and deeply haunted by the
latter. Philosopher that I am, I am committed for
what I consider good resons to the search for truth
through reason and empirical evidence. When I try
to render coherent the whole phenomenon of our
poetic ways of relating ourselves to the world, I
become utterly baffled in the face of their variety,
confusion, and contradictions and retreat once again
to the safer and solider ground of rational-
empirical knowledge. When, for example, Charlie
speaks vaguely and generally of "the poets" as
revealers of being, which ones does he mean? Plato
or Lucretius? Shakespeare or Milton? Poe or
Whitman? Eliot or Stevens? Surely he cannot make
them all witnesses to the soul and transcendence--or
can he? and if so, how? But the conviction that
amid the welter and cacophony there is something
profoundly real disclosed in those imaginings and
intuitings that are so dominant in our lives will
not let me go even though discursively I have
absolutely no idea what to make of it. Perhaps in
imaginative-intuitive modes of apprehension and
relationship "soul" and "immortality" acquire
meanings and reality which they lack on the

rational-empirical level; meanings and reality which simply elude and transcend conceptual analysis. I simply do not know.

One thing I believe the "argument from absurdity" highlights is that naturalistic no less than transcendental accounts of ourselves and the world are finally <u>decisions</u> about how to interpret experience for which reasons are necessary but not, I think, sufficient. For the data of our experience are richly textured, complex, and ambiguous; they lend themselves to various sorts of interpretation. For this reason Charlie Citrine's struggle with the either/or, the finally unrationalizable choice between what we will accept as authentic and inauthentic in our knowledge and relationship to reality, has vigorously stimulated in me a new struggling with the baffling epistemological issue of alternative world-perspectives.

Aristotle may turn out to have been right after all when he wrote that "nature does nothing in vain." It is at least plausible, in the light of the seeming "vanity"--that is, the apparent futility--of so many human desires and imaginings within our physical context, to consider that "nature" may be more than we know. A fictional character named Charlie Citrine has disturbed me with yet another reminder of the nagging possibility that, in the words of Hamlet, "there are more things in heaven and earth than are dreamt of in our philosophy."

Having begun this book with despair over the problem of God in the light of human bondage, I end with a certain groping, hopeful perplexity over the possibility of transcendence precisely by looking at our bondage from yet another perspective. I have drawn again on the Augustinian tradition as it expresses itself in the "argument from absurdity," this time by way of haltingly grappling with the fact that even within a skeptical humanistic perspective one can and ought to be profoundly haunted by the possibility that we in our mysterious bondage and our darkly enveloping cosmic environment may be far more than we know or suspect except through the terribly inadequate symbols of faith. Both the despair and the hope seem to me to belong

to a humanism that tries to be sensitive to the full
complexity of human experience.

FOOTNOTES

[1] N.Y.: Avon, 1975. Page references from _Humboldt's Gift_ will appear in parentheses in the text of the paper.

[2] Trans. Rowe Portis, Phila.: University of Pennsylvania Press, 1969.

[3] Camus's most explicit development of the theme of absurdity is of course _The Myth of Sisyphus_ (trans. by Justin O'Brien, N.Y.: Knopf, 1955). The above discussion appears in the section on "An Absurd Reasoning," pp. 3-48.

[4] Thomas Aquinas furnishes a typical example of this sort of appeal. In the _Summa Contra Gentiles_ he argues, in his characteristically crisp and syllogistic fashion, for the truth of immortality on the basis of "natural desire": "Natural desire cannot be empty, since _nature does nothing in vain_ [Aristotle]. But nature's desire would be empty if it could never be fulfilled. Therefore man's natural desire [for happiness] can be fulfilled. But not in this life, as we have shown. Therefore it must be fulfilled after this life. Therefore man's ultimate happiness is after this life." (Anton C. Pegis, ed., _Introduction to Saint Thomas Aquinas_, N.Y.: Modern Library, 1948, p. 466).

[5] Vol. II, Trans. by Walter Lowrie with revisions and a foreword by Howard A. Johnson, Garden City: Anchor, 1959, p. 167.

135

[6] *Fear and Trembling and The Sickness Unto Death*, trans. with Introductions and Notes by Walter Lowrie, Garden City: Anchor, 1954, pp. 159-160.

[7] *Bright Shadow of Reality: C. S. Lewis and the Feeling Intellect*, Grand Rapids: Eerdmans, 1974, p. 15. My italics.

[8] P. 23. My italics.

[9] I hasten to add that the central image of sleep in Charlie's reflections is a vigorously paradoxical one. In general, when he speaks of sleep in a figurative sense, he is referring to his own and humankind's inauthentic condition of ignorance about who we really are. But when he discusses literal sleep, he takes the view that our deepest intimations about and contacts with higher realities occur during this natural unconscious state, as e.g. in prophetic and poetic inspiration from dream states. Part of the tragedy of modern life is that one expression of our captivity to the Big Sleep of despairing ignorance is our inability to sleep in such a way as to be open to these profounder intimations.

[10] *Forgotten Truth: The Primordial Tradition*, N.Y.: Harper & Row, 1976.

[11] *Dynamics of Faith*, N.Y.: Harper & Brothers, 1957, p. 42.

[12] *Tragic Sense of Life*, trans. by J. E. Crawford Flitch, N.Y.: Dover, 1954, p. 259. One limitation of Unamuno's view is of course his notion of immortality as "an endless continuation of our earthly life"--a relentlessly literalistic notion which neither Charlie nor Steiner, neither Platonism nor Christianity, hold.